Making pressed flower pictures

Also published by Batsford:

Pressed Flowers through the Seasons, Margaret Kennedy Scott &
Mary Beazley, 1983

Pressed Wild Flower Pictures, Mary Beazley, 1985

Making pressed flower pictures

**Margaret Kennedy Scott
and Mary Beazley**

B T Batsford Ltd London

The authors wish to acknowledge the help
of John Sayer in photographing some of
the colour plates, and A C Cooper Ltd in
photographing the black and white photo-
graphs. The line illustrations were drawn
by Margaret Kennedy Scott.

First published 1979
First published in paperback 1981
Reprinted 1982, 1983, 1985, 1987

ISBN 0 7134 5771 6 (paperback)

Printed and bound in Great Britain by
Anchor Brendon Ltd, Tiptree, Essex
for the publishers B T Batsford Limited
4 Fitzhardinge Street, London W1H 0AH

Contents

Introduction

We have been making pressed flower pictures for many years and during this time we have met a number of people who asked us to explain exactly how we do it. 'I must try it myself' is the phrase we often hear. We hope that this book will inspire the beginner to take up this attractive and rewarding craft, and that our designs will help those who are already making pictures to enlarge their own store of ideas.

Both of us make flower pictures for fun and for sale. We are drawn into different aspects of the craft: one makes pictures for craft markets and so helps in the revival of country crafts, while the other teaches adult students how to make flower pictures as a recreational subject. We find there is an inexhaustible source of inspiration in flowers and leaves. Sometimes this will find expression in the creation of large and elegant pictures, and sometimes in delicate cards and small designs.

We have included in this book all the basic techniques and information about the preparation and pressing of flowers. We give suggestions about frames and backgrounds and have devoted a large section to the actual construction of good, basic designs.

Making flower pictures is an extremely rewarding hobby: not only is it satisfying to learn how to acquire a delicate skill with your fingers, but there is the added attraction of broadening your knowledge of flowers and plants.

We have tried to make this book as wide-ranging as possible — wild flowers from the countryside are included as well as garden flowers. Full information is given on the suitability of each type of plant, which blooms and leaves will press better than others, and how to avoid pitfalls and errors. Very simple cards and pictures are dealt with as fully as the most intricate flower compositions in the more elaborate frames. The chapters are arranged so that you can start literally from the beginning and by obtaining the materials given in the lists in the opening chapters you can steadily build up your confidence in choosing, handling and pressing flowers, and making them into increasingly more advanced pictures. It is not difficult, and we guarantee that by the time you have completed your first picture you will be longing to start another.

Flowers and presses

EQUIPMENT

Small polythene (plastic) box and lid
Simple books on wild flowers and garden flowers
Small secateurs (pruning shears)
Tweezers (eyebrow tweezers with straight ends are ideal)
Press (bought or home-made)
Two pieces of hardboard the same size as the press (where required)
Blotting paper (white or coloured)
Scissors (straight nail scissors are ideal)
Craft knife (such as a Stanley, Exacto or X-acto knife)
Newspapers

The two major things to consider in the initial stages are efficiency and cost, and you will find that the equipment needed for pressing flowers is relatively cheap. Expensive flowers and prize blooms are no better for making pictures than the average ones, and, even if you have no garden, wild flowers, leaves and grasses are there for the picking. Even in towns and cities one can find small flowers growing on waste ground, and, to start with, the amount one needs to pick need not be very great.

The flower press is the most important part of your equipment, and here again you will not have to pay out a great deal of money; on the whole home-made flower presses or second-hand old-fashioned presses for trousers and slacks are more efficient than the expensive custom-made variety bought in shops.

COLLECTING FLOWERS

You can collect flowers, leaves, grasses and seed heads for pressing in almost any month of the year, and the only golden rule which you must obey is not to pick and press when it is raining or misty. Damp specimens are susceptible to mould while in the press. On the whole the overblown flower does not keep its colour, so try to pick only the freshly opened blooms. Collect the specimens in a basket or loose bag and protect them from being bruised or broken; small buds or tendrils are obviously very vulnerable. Try to cut down the time between cutting and pressing, for the

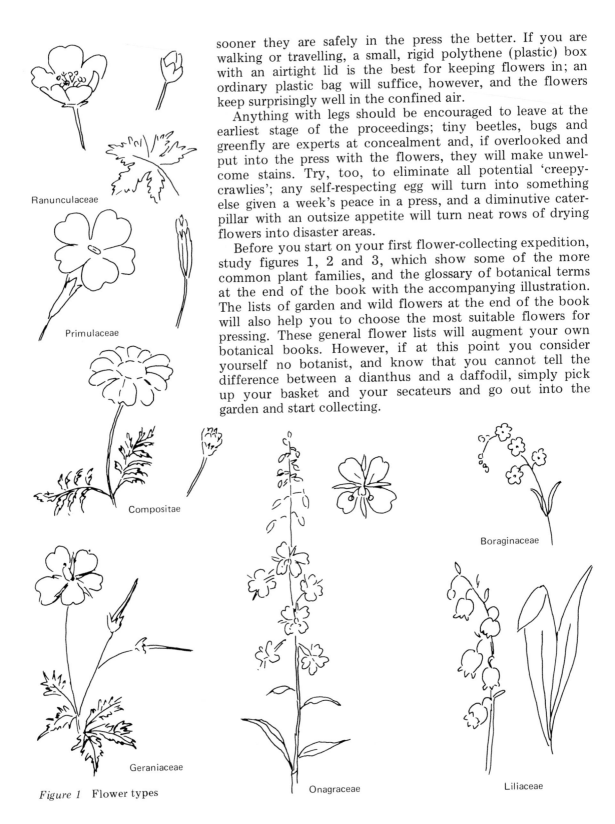

sooner they are safely in the press the better. If you are walking or travelling, a small, rigid polythene (plastic) box with an airtight lid is the best for keeping flowers in; an ordinary plastic bag will suffice, however, and the flowers keep surprisingly well in the confined air.

Anything with legs should be encouraged to leave at the earliest stage of the proceedings; tiny beetles, bugs and greenfly are experts at concealment and, if overlooked and put into the press with the flowers, they will make unwelcome stains. Try, too, to eliminate all potential 'creepy-crawlies'; any self-respecting egg will turn into something else given a week's peace in a press, and a diminutive caterpillar with an outsize appetite will turn neat rows of drying flowers into disaster areas.

Before you start on your first flower-collecting expedition, study figures 1, 2 and 3, which show some of the more common plant families, and the glossary of botanical terms at the end of the book with the accompanying illustration. The lists of garden and wild flowers at the end of the book will also help you to choose the most suitable flowers for pressing. These general flower lists will augment your own botanical books. However, if at this point you consider yourself no botanist, and know that you cannot tell the difference between a dianthus and a daffodil, simply pick up your basket and your secateurs and go out into the garden and start collecting.

Ranunculaceae

Primulaceae

Compositae

Boraginaceae

Geraniaceae

Onagraceae

Liliaceae

Figure 1 Flower types

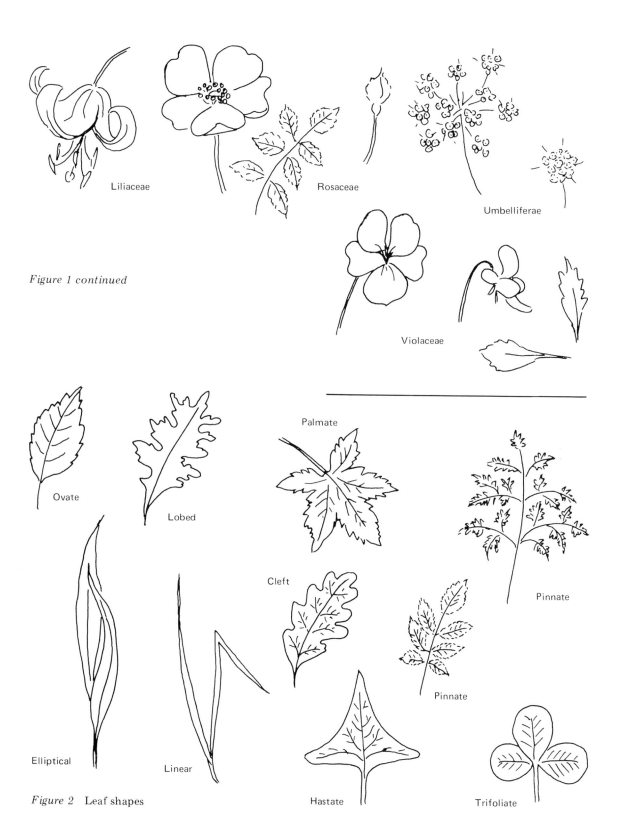

Liliaceae

Rosaceae

Umbelliferae

Figure 1 continued

Violaceae

Ovate

Lobed

Palmate

Cleft

Pinnate

Pinnate

Elliptical

Linear

Hastate

Trifoliate

Figure 2 Leaf shapes

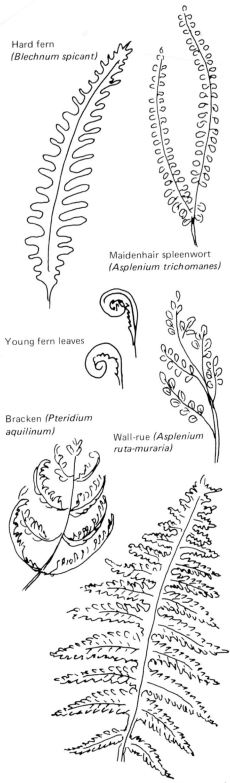

Hard fern
(Blechnum spicant)

Maidenhair spleenwort
(Asplenium trichomanes)

Young fern leaves

Bracken (Pteridium
aquilinum)

Wall-rue (Asplenium
ruta-muraria)

Lady fern (Athyrium filix-femina)

Figure 3 Fern types

Wander along the hedgerows and pick some of the wild flowers, kneel down in the grass and consider carefully some of the small flowers you had always dismissed as weeds before. Look at the buds and the seed heads, look for tendrils and curly stems, notice the shape of the leaves and ferns and whether there is much variation in the colour of the old ones as compared to the new. Cast your eye on the shrubs and trees too, for you are entering your familiar garden from a new angle; there are treasures here which you have never considered as such before.

When gathering wild flowers in the countryside, however, remember to leave plenty of flower heads on the plants in any given area, so that the species may continue to propagate there. In the UK, it is an offence to uproot (i.e. dig up) any wild plant without the permission of the landowner. Some species which are in danger of becoming extinct are protected by law in the British Isles, and the removal of any part of these plants is forbidden. A list of plants currently protected by the Act is given at the end of the book.

Points to remember

1 Do not collect damaged, torn or old specimens.
2 Do not collect wet flowers or leaves.
3 Thick flowers and seed heads are difficult to press.
4 Always try to identify specimens while they are fresh.

FLOWER PRESSES

The most important requirement of a flower press is that it should exert a heavy and uniform pressure; the colour and shape of specimens are preserved best when they are pressed tightly. The absorbent material above and beneath will soak up the moisture from the crushed plant tissues, and the more quickly this is done the better. There are various methods of pressing flowers, ranging from the traditional school exercise-book to the expensive, custom-built flower press from a craft shop, but there is no mystique about any of them — most methods will work. Given two pieces of fairly absorbent paper, some flower heads and a heavy book, the drying and pressing process will take place; but if you want a wide selection of perfect specimens to use in picture making, it will be advisable for you to discard the old newspaper, the paper handkerchieves and the telephone directory, and choose one of the following well-tried methods.

The heavy book

Choose a large book — not a valuable one — and preferably one that is not smaller than 30 cm x 22 cm (12 in. x 9 in.). Take a half-sheet of standard-sized blotting paper and fold it in two, so that you have a folder just a little smaller than the book. Place the folder inside the book so that the fold of the blotting paper lies along the spine of the book and it opens with the book. Take several more folded blotting-paper sheets and place them in the same manner at regular intervals throughout the book, making sure that they are separated from each other by ten or more pages. You now have a number of blotting-paper folders ready to receive the flowers, but before you begin, collect together a pile of really heavy books which you can place on top as a weight — the heavier the better.

Two trays

You will need two rigid household trays, one a little smaller than the other so that it fits inside it, and some blotting paper. The foot of a heavy piece of furniture, such as a bed, can be used as the force that exerts the pressure to flatten the flowers. (It is unwise to use one's own bed for this purpose since the sharp corner of the trays protruding into the room would present something of a hazard, particularly in the dark. The bed in the guest room is recommended.)

Take the larger of the two trays and lay a folded sheet of newspaper on it, then take a sheet of blotting paper and put this on top. Fold the paper down to fit the tray if it is too big, or trim the corners with scissors. Prepare several sheets of blotting paper and some newspaper layers, then find a flat, strong, thin piece of wood about 15 cm (6 in.) wide and a little shorter than the smaller tray; this will be used as a stretcher on top of the two trays and under one foot of the bed. It is possible to use two pieces of hardboard pressed together in the same manner as trays, but the latter are recommended because the upright edges of the bottom tray will keep dust away from the flowers.

Trouser press

Old-fashioned presses for trousers and slacks can be bought cheaply from jumble sales, charity shops and sale rooms. There are basically two varieties, the simple screw-down one and the more complicated lever type, and there is no doubt that the former is the best. With four strong butter-fly nuts, a sound wooden base, slatted wood top, and the whole reinforced by solid metal strips, it is ideal for pressing flowers. The lever types, however, were built solely for creasing gentlemen's trousers, and they tend to bulge and give way when offered a diet of blotting paper and flower sandwiches more than 5 cm (2 in.) in width.

Having brought home your ready-made press in triumph, you will need to assemble two or three pieces of hardboard of the same size, some newspapers and a good pile of blotting paper cut to size. Make sure that the press is clean — a little grease on the threads of the screws will help when the nuts have to be tightened. These presses are very heavy and cumbersome when full.

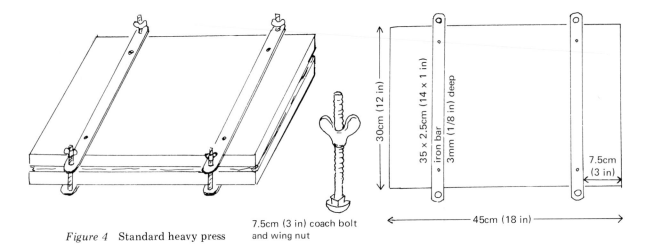

Figure 4 Standard heavy press

7.5cm (3 in) coach bolt and wing nut

Making a heavy press

A flower press is not difficult to make. In design it is similar to the old trouser-press variety, and you can make it at home with the minimum of assistance and the co-operation of the local hardware store.

You will need two rectangular pieces of 1.25 cm (½ in.) chipboard (thick, lightweight wooden board made from compressed wood chips). If the half-sheet of blotting paper you are using measures 44 cm x 29 cm (17½ in. x 11½ in.), cut the chipboard to measure 45 cm x 30 cm (18 in. x 12 in.) or ask your dealer to cut it to size for you. You will also need four narrow strips of metal, preferably of iron, but essentially strong enough not to bend under pressure, four coach bolts 7.5 cm (3 in.) long and four wing-nuts. (Coach bolts have domed tops, and are therefore safer to use than the ordinary hexagonal-topped bolts.) These metal strips can be obtained at the local hardware store and need to be about 2.5 cm (1 in.) wide, 35 cm (14 in.) long and 3 mm (⅛ in.) thick. Ask the dealer to bore holes through them into which the coach bolts will fit snugly, the holes being placed 1.25 cm (½ in.) in from each end. Two further screw holes should be bored in each strip so that they may be fixed to the chipboard by ordinary 1.25 cm (½ in.) screws, and these should be about 7.5 cm (3 in.) in from the ends as shown in figure 4. This procedure must be repeated with the second piece of chipboard. The coach bolts are passed through the holes at the ends of the strips, and, as the wing-nuts are tightened, the boards will be pressed together. Collect together some sheets of blotting paper, a few pieces of similar-sized hardboard and old newspapers to fit, and the press is ready for the flowers.

Travelling presses

Tie press

The large books and wooden tea-trays, angular trouser presses and the excellent heavy model, alive with aggressive bolt ends, are understandably uncomfortable companions on holiday, and it is worthwhile investing in a lightweight smaller press such as a tie press, which will not take up much room in a suitcase. It is simply no use imagining that once you have really started collecting flowers your new-found craze can be ignored while you are on holiday in some beautiful place with the flowers nodding round your feet! The unfamiliar or bright exotic blossoms may well turn this modest interest into a mania, and it is then that this small press will come into its own; your hotel bedroom will be littered with flowers to identify and press, and only the unwanted stalks will be consigned eventually to the wastepaper basket.

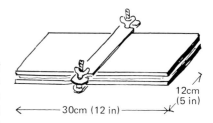

Figure 5 Tie press

Plywood press

An excellent travelling press can be made by using lightweight Mersawa plywood. (Plywood is made up of thin layers of wood, the grains of which run at right angles to each other.) You need two rectangles, each measuring 27 cm x 33 cm (10½ in. x 13 in.). This takes a half-sheet of blotting paper folded down to 22 cm x 29 cm (8½ in. x 11½ in.) and allows for the coach-bolt holes to be drilled 7.5 cm (3 in.) from the ends of the longer sides. The holes need to be inset as far as this to ensure that the thin plywood does not warp when the bolts are screwed down on a full press. The coach bolts for this press should be only 6.4 cm (2½ in.) long with, of course, the appropriate wing-nuts. Two pieces of hardboard cut to the same size are also required.

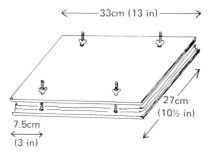

Figure 6 Plywood travelling press

Commercial flower presses

You can buy various sizes of flower presses from most department stores and from good craft supply shops. They consist usually of two squares of lightweight wood, four small drilled holes in the corners, with four thin screws and wing-nuts, and a generous supply of fitted blotting paper and thick card interleaves. These will press your specimens efficiently, but the task of threading and unthreading the light screws can be very time-consuming when you have small numbers of specimens to go into the press at a time, as for example on holiday. Moreover, the size of these presses is unlikely to be as satisfactory for heavy work as the larger ones suggested earlier in the chapter. For these reasons, commerical presses are not recommended as highly as the types mentioned above.

15

The lunatic fringe

Most enthusiasts are a little eccentric about some aspect of their own particular hobby — and flower-pressing devotees are no exception. Treasured is the recollection of the student who came to evening class with three tennis-racket presses under her arm. There were no long handles sticking out behind her, only familiar folds of white blotting paper where the rackets should have been. What of the friend coming home from Greece who had a very awkward time revealing to the Customs the bulging roll of lavatory paper and the flowers going round and round inside like crazy writing in a giant stick of rock!

The time-honoured method used by many enthusiasts is also worth remembering. Slip the blotting paper with the flowers between sheets of newspaper and slide the whole thing under the carpet, choosing the part of the house which most resembles a busy railway station, and the tramp, tramp, tramp of family feet will do the rest.

Blotting paper

This should preferably be white since this shows up the fine details of shape and outline when one comes to select a flower for a particular position. Buy it in bulk if you can; you will certainly need more than you think and it is cheaper this way. A quire (24 sheets) is usually quoted as the minimum wholesale quantity, and normally you will divide each sheet into two. Shop around — there is considerable variation in price. You should be able to get blotting paper from most good stationers, both retail and wholesale.

Storage of presses

Do not store a press in a place which collects dust, such as under the bed; if using the foot of the bed as a weight, ensure that the press is well covered. Dampness is also damaging both to the press and the specimens. If possible, store the press in a warm, dry cupboard, avoiding direct heat which might cause the wood to warp and split. Remember that a full press is very heavy, so take care when lifting it.

Pressing flowers

PREPARATION

The proverbial joke about the man building a wall with a brick in one hand and the instruction book in the other might well introduce this chapter, since this — mainly a practical operation — will rely on neat fingers and common sense. So keep this book in front of you and set up a table with your new press, plenty of blotting paper, scissors and the flowers you have picked.

The number of flowers that you might possibly pick throughout the year is immense. The blossoms vary greatly in size and style, the colour range is spectacular, and their ebullient complexity is a far cry from the simplicity of design of the final flower picture. One might be forgiven for thinking that Nature left to herself is always trying to crowd in as much detail as possible, while Art is equally determined in her attempt to leave it out. It is obvious that a large flower-packed mass transported straight from the garden would make a poor foundation for a picture if it were all put into the press without some initial discrimination and some work with the scissors to prune it down.

Some flowers will press well, some are unreliable, and there is a small minority which is not worth putting into the press at all. Colour will stay or fade according to the species, and some flowers will change colour completely. For example, *Galium verum* (Lady's bedstraw) will go black and *Lithospermum diffusum* (Heavenly blue) usually turns pink. Some leaves will shrivel and fade, while others will appear even sharper in outline when they are dry. Multiply these factors by the numbers of flowers at your disposal, consider the size of your press and the amount of time you can spare, and you will realize how important it is that you press only specimens with a good drying potential. Nothing is more depressing than finding that one has compiled pages of dried unusable leaves, and flowers that are shapeless, giving only pale echoes of their true colours, with all their clear and individual beauty lost and your time and enthusiasm wasted.

Experience is a very slow way to discover which flowers and leaves retain their colour and shape best. This chapter gives sound advice in this matter, and will help to save time and disappointment.

COLOUR

This should be the first consideration because the eye will be attracted by it immediately. Violet, indigo, blue, green, yellow, orange and red is the run of colours in the spectrum. The first two are easy to preserve; all shades of mauve and violet will retain their colour, willow-herb and violas being some of the best examples. Indigo, that dark blue-purple you find in larkspur and woody nightshade (bittersweet), can be a fast colour, but the nearer it approaches the true blue that we find in the harebell and forget-me-not, the more unreliable it will be. Blue is the most fugitive of the colours, and offers the most disappointments, for in the pages of dried blue flowers there will be a number of faded specimens varying from fawn to dirty blue; but the ones that have retained their strong pure colour will be of great value when you come to make a picture.

Green, of course, is the colour produced by the chemical chlorophyll, and on the whole it will be held in the dried leaves, calyx and flowers very well. Beware of leaves with shiny surfaces like the variegated ivy, because the green will sometimes fade to beige. Yellows and oranges are probably the most permanent — carotene being fairly stable chemically — and all flowers of these colours from buttercups to anthemis will be beautiful when they are dried.

Red again is a suspect colour, since it can sometimes dry a dark, brownish shade which is not always attractive, and the flamboyant scarlet of a geranium will often fade to fawn. Yet a well-preserved wallflower can be a splendid focal point in a picture, and with the help of the detailed glossaries at the end of the book you should achieve considerable success in pressing red flowers.

White flowers will dry well, some retaining a startling brilliance, and when they lose a little brightness in drying the gentle creamy shade will still give you pleasure.

Silver foliage will dry true in colour, and at the other end of the colour scale there are some green leaves which will dry a dark green bordering on black. Most autumn-tinted leaves also are happy to keep their reds and golds after weeks in the press, so there is certainly a tremendous range of colour in foliage as well as in flower heads.

Never attempt to dye flowers, and beware of the ones you may acquire from florists which have already been dipped: the artificial colours will not fade and mellow at the same rate as the natural ones. After a period of time these artificially dyed flowers will appear harsh and crude in amongst the undyed flowers. The normal mellowing of the natural colours will simply appear as fading, and the overall balance and charm will have been lost.

SHAPE

It is essential to look carefully at the shape of the specimens and to consider not only the height and width of the flowers and leaves but also the third dimension, the depth. Look down on the top of the plant and you will see straight away the pattern of branching stems. Leaves, flowers and buds frequently emanate all round the clock, as it were, and you will be aware of the problems and complexities of growth shape in pressing. You are aiming for the nearly two-dimensional pressed flower, and you will have to trim carefully before you can put specimens into the press. This trimming will apply whether you are dealing with a long stalk comprising several flower heads and leaves or with a single blossom.

With the former type of specimen, first stand it up on its stalk, look down on it, decide which is the best side, and turn this towards you. Notice which are the lateral shoots on this plane. Leave these on the plant, but either gently bend sideways or carefully detach the stems and leaves which grow towards you or away from you (figure 7).

Exactly the same selection process will apply to the single blossom which you want to press full face. The stem of the flower should be cut out as close to the calyx as possible, otherwise the dried stem will leave a dent on the face of the flower, and this will show in the finished picture. To cut off the unwanted parts, hold the flower firmly by means of the tweezers and gently snip at the trumpet or calyx with the sharp, pointed scissors (figure 8).

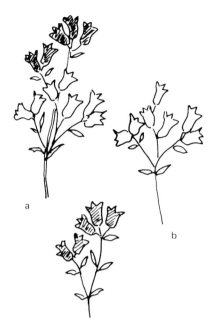

Figure 7 Removing the upper stem of heuchera which has grown on a different plane from that of the lower stem

Figure 8 Removing the trumpet or calyx from a single flower

Figure 9 Cut and press the stamens, pistil and petals of a passion flower separately

A passion flower will need to have the pistil and stamens removed before pressing, and then all three parts can be placed together again when they are dry (figure 9). Although you can cut off the small florets of the umbelliferae family (figure 10), such as cow parsley, and dry each one separately, beware of using the same treatment on the dianthus, such as sweetwilliam, and also on the compositae family, for too rigorous a cutting away of the deep calyx will mean that all the petals will fall off. Common sense really dictates the preparation of flowers for the press and will help to avoid failures. Flowers that have considerable depth like delphinium and larkspur can be pressed in profile very successfully. The narcissus can also be pressed full face if the trumpet is first slit into several 'petals' (figure 12).

Figure 10 Press some umbelliferae heads complete; cut florets off others and press singly

STRUCTURE

The basic structure of a plant often determines how well it will dry. Fibrous plants like flax and anaphalis are excellent, while succulents and fleshy-leaved types are disappointing. The water content will soak into the blotting paper and there will be little left of the original shape and colour. Orchids and African violets will usually fail for this

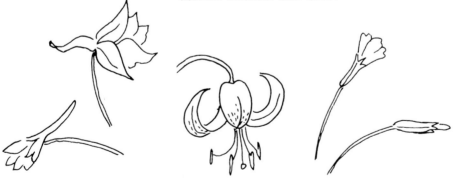

Figure 11 The delphinium, lily and primrose press well in profile

reason. Shiny leaves are slow to dry and the hairy varieties like *Stachys lanata* are easily ruffled in the press; both types of leaves need extra care.

Seed heads and buds are frequently well worth pressing. Often they are too solid to put into the press as they are, so try cutting them in half lengthways with a craft knife (holding them in the tweezers so that your fingers are well away from the knife). These will dry successfully — and you will get two for the price of one. A very unlikely fruit that will charm you with its dried appearance is the half-formed wild strawberry. Put a few of these in your picture, and you will be forgiven for thinking that, with the addition of a butterfly and a small flattened beetle, you are in the same league as Jan van Huysum.

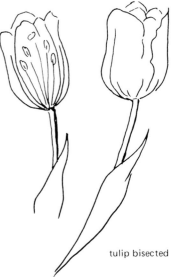

Figure 12 Slitting the trumpet of the narcissus

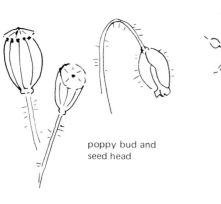

alyssum seed head

poppy bud and seed head

wild strawberry

Figure 13 Seed heads and buds

tulip bisected

PRESSING

Flowers should be fresh, young and dry; discard the damaged specimens. When laying the flowers on the blotting paper, it is often best to place them face downwards.

1 Lay a fresh sheet of blotting paper in your open press.
2 Trim and tidy the flowers and leaves, and lay them in rows on the blotting paper: head to tail is usually the most space saving. Do not let them touch.
3 Place some full face and some profile if possible. (Some varieties will only lie one way; for example, lily of the valley lies in profile, and an open *Clematis montana* lies full face.)
4 Place all the leaves, small stalks, buds, and tendrils from one plant on the same page.
5 Press more specimens than you think you will need — the surplus will allow for some early failures.

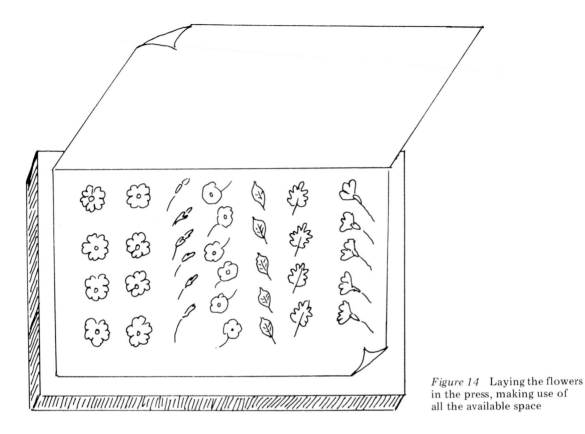

Figure 14 Laying the flowers in the press, making use of all the available space

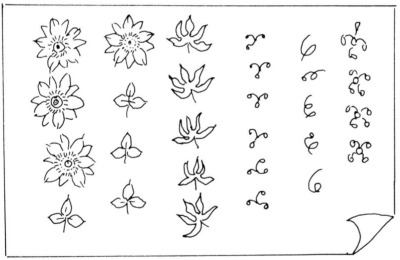

Figure 15 All the separated parts of each flower should be placed on the same layer

6 When the first page is full, cover it with a fresh sheet and start again.

7 After each two sheets of blotting paper have been used, put in a double sheet of newspaper.

8 Try to press thin textured specimens on one layer, and

22

thicker flowers on another, so that an equal pressure is applied over all the specimens.

9 Make a note of the date and where the flowers came from on the last sheet before you screw the press down.

This last point is most important when you are pressing flowers for a special occasion, such as from a bride's wedding bouquet. Bride A will not be pleased if she receives a picture of bride B's flowers by mistake, and vice versa, so always label the flowers clearly. When you get a press full of flowers, intersperse the blotting paper with two sheets of thin hardboard, to ensure that the layers do not become distorted and so ruin the shape of the flowers. Screw the press down very firmly. As the moisture dries the screws will loosen, so you should tighten them down every day until they will screw no further.

SORTING AND TURNING

The length of time that is needed to dry and press flowers fully depends on the type of press being used, where it is being stored, and the type of specimens. Thin-textured flowers screwed down tightly in a warm place will be dry in two weeks or even less, but the thicker varieties, such as members of the daisy family or the rose, will take up to six weeks. When flowers are ready to be used, they will be completely dry, the petals paper thin and brittle.

With the thicker type of material you should open the press after five or six days and very carefully lift and turn the flowers. Always use the tweezers to pick up the flowers. You may well think after an initial failure or two that your fingers would do the job better, but resist this temptation at all costs, since the petals will be too brittle to withstand handling. It takes only a very short time to master the use of the tweezers, and later on in the delicate work of making a picture their use will be essential.

The small areas of blotting paper on which these half-dried flowers have been lying may be a little damp, so be careful to move each flower onto a dry area. If you omit to turn these thick flower heads, they may gradually stick to the paper in drying, so that when you eventually try to lift them off they will break and the thin petals will come away.

Another reason for checking the flowers at this point is that you can prevent any mould from forming. Always discard any specimen that appears to be harbouring this, for it is easily recognizable, appearing as a greenish-white or greenish-black moist dust on and around the flowers. If left for a few weeks unattended it will spread through an entire layer. It has an unpleasant musty smell, and the flowers will turn black and be quite unusable. Mould usually attacks flowers stored in damp conditions, and provided you

five-petalled flower

daisy shape

many-petalled flower

many-headed flower

never press wet flowers you should not be troubled. As a safety precaution you should keep your press in a warm place, such as a heated linen cupboard.

After this initial turning and sorting, screw the press down tightly again. It is quite a good idea to put it somewhere where you pass by frequently and can give the nuts an extra twist or two. The perfect flower specimen is a *hard*-pressed flower.

STORING PRESSED FLOWERS

Before you take all the specimens out of the press, think ahead about the best way of storing them to save yourself time and energy when you come to make a picture. Remember that bright sunlight will fade the natural colours in flowers in exactly the same way that it will a watercolour painting. Flower pictures should always be hung facing away from the light. Similarly, when you are storing flowers, keep them out of the sun as much as possible.

It is sensible to decide from the outset whether you want your material sorted into colours, species or by size. This must be entirely a personal choice, but it must be a consistent one, because if the flowers are just thrown together into a container you will certainly damage them unnecessarily when you come to search through them for a particular size or shape.

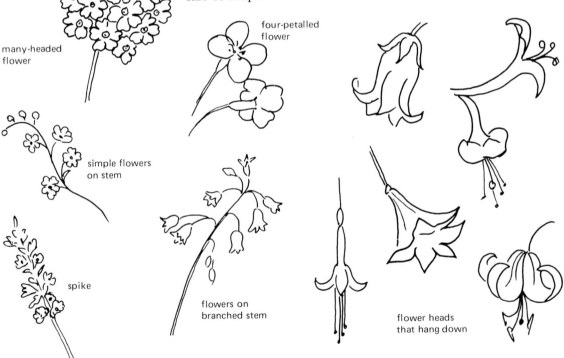

four-petalled flower

simple flowers on stem

spike

flowers on branched stem

flower heads that hang down

Figure 16 Categorizing the flower shapes

1 Small wild and garden flowers make up the designs in these little pictures. The two
   gold frames are modern, and the others are Victorian – one with an unusual
   convex glass

2 Diminutive flowers, buds, ferns and grasses have been used in these greetings
cards, framed by hand-inked borders

Filing system

Take a double sheet of fresh blotting paper, fold it in half, lay it on a flat surface, and place the dry specimens in between the folds. Take a small tab of card, write on it the details of the flowers, and attach it (with adhesive tape or a staple) to the top corner of the blotting-paper file. With the next sheet attach the name tab a little further along from the corner. Continue in this manner and you will soon have made yourself a well catalogued flower library.

It is essential that any flower or leaf over 1.25 cm (½ in.) in diameter should be kept flat between two surfaces, otherwise the edges of the specimens will curl up and the flower will be spoiled.

Flower chest

Small sets of very shallow drawers are also excellent for storing specimens. Dentist's cabinets, cardboard stationery drawers and egg-collector's cabinets are all useful for storing small flowers and leaves.

Remember that you will need at least seven different containers or files, whichever method you decide on; separation by colour alone (violet, indigo, blue, green, yellow, orange and red) would require this basic number. Always use the tweezers when moving the flowers, and never throw away any little pieces of stem and foliage if they are in good condition, since they may well be useful in completing a design.

Frames

TOOLS AND MATERIALS

Some or all of the following equipment will be required for general frame repairs and for making small frames.

Small pliers (pointed)
Small hammer
Small saw (such as a tenon saw)
Drill
Mitre block and clamp (or mitre clamps)
Vice (or vise)
Two small good-quality paint brushes 1.25 cm (½ in.) or 2 cm (¾ in.)
Veneer pins (0.5 cm (¼ in.), 1.25 cm (½ in.) or 1.5 cm ($^5/_8$ in.) depending on the width of the moulding)
Sandpaper of varying grades (for stripping large frames, M2 followed by 01; for smaller mouldings and angle joins, F2 followed by 01; 'flourpaper' for all fine surfaces)
Woodwork adhesive
Plastic wood
Plastic padding
Strong, smooth running string or cord
Spray paints
Gold paint (such as 'Classic' or 'Renaissance Gold')
Gold wax polish
Artist's oil paints, small tubes of Vandyke Brown and Burnt Umber
White spirit
Old rags, newspapers
Guillotine (paper cutter) or sharp craft knife
Steel rule

(Opposite)
A maple wood frame, stripped, waxed and polished to give a soft sheen, makes a suitable setting for this vase of flowers on a dark brown silk background. The container is a golden day lily which tones beautifully with the colour of the frame. The flowers are soft mixed colours: pale blue hydrangeas and scillas, cream primroses and narcissus with crimson potentillas.

CHOICE OF FRAME

The choice of frame must be the first consideration in making a flower picture; cost alone would usually dictate this, and the overall design must complement the frame in which it is to be presented. A picture is composed of flowers and leaves mounted on a harmonious background, surrounded by a frame of the appropriate size, style and colour. The picture must be designed as a whole, but the focus must ultimately rest on the flowers.

Victorian metal frame

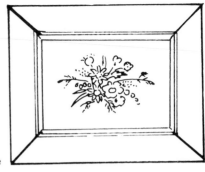
antique maple wood frame

antique gilt moulded frame

frame made of narrow plain moulding

Figure 17 Different types of frame

It would be unrealistic to ignore the question of cost; really top-quality frames incorporating expert craftsmanship are expensive and increase in price every year. However, they can be a wise choice when making a picture for a specialist market as the value will increase over the years. The range in cost from the simple wood frame to the antique gold one is wide, and should allow the beginner to buy an inexpensive frame and still be pleased with the result. Always bear in mind the fact that a picture frame should enclose and present the central theme with just the correct amount of definition.

There are so many different types of moulding for frames, and different mixtures of colours, golds and ornamentation, that it can be extremely bewildering to choose one in preference to all the others, and this dilemma will assail you whether you purchase a ready-made frame or buy moulding in lengths and have it made up. Beware the baroque, the heavy, ornate mouldings, or the bright, gaudy frame. Teamed up with even the most colourful flowers, you will have 'a four-cornered sensation with something in the middle' to start with, and after a year or two and a little gentle fading you will be left with a visual disaster. Growing old gracefully applies just as much to the mellowed flowers of a picture as it does to the female face; frames and hairstyles should subtly flatter and enhance nature, not annihilate it.

Consider the question of size carefully. Obviously a monster frame about a metre (3 ft.) square will not enhance small rosebuds and lilies of the valley very successfully — even with a clematis or two to fill the space. So before you decide that 'Big is Beautiful' and that you must fill such an enormous challenge, pause and reflect on how you are going to press and store the outsize specimens, the emperor ferns and the chestnut leaves. Common sense suggests caution in this matter of overall size, for usually it is wisest to play safe, and to leave the double poppies in the herbaceous border, the heavy roses to the wallpaper manufacturer, and the sunflowers to the parrots. Simplicity of frame is frequently the best, and the range of size most suited to the flowers you can most practically press and store will probably lie between 12 cm (5 in.) and 30 cm (12 in.) square.

Frames can be acquired in several different ways, and although at first you may just go out to the nearest shop and buy one, after making a few pictures you will certainly want to add to your store in other ways and build up a good collection of frames with a variety of styles.

ANTIQUE FRAMES

There is no doubt at all that a fine, antique oval frame around a good arrangement of pressed flowers in the traditional style, mounted on a pure silk background, is a thing of beauty. Old gilt and fine wood frames of the right size are now becoming difficult to find and increasingly expensive to buy, but large-sized, good-quality frames can still be bought at sales and in antique shops, and these can be successfully cut down to make smaller frames.

Sale-room 'bundling' normally dictates how many you will have to buy in a 'lot', so you should be prepared for several 'Views of the Highlands', 'Venice in the 1890s' and depressingly sentimental pictures of dogs all framed in heavy oak or coloured composition frames, just for the sake of acquiring one bird's-eye-maple wood frame. But the sorting, the bidding and the taking home of the spoils are fun, and in the acquisition of attractive, good-quality frames you will be well rewarded.

Antique shops, local bazaars, sales and junk shops are all worth visiting in your quest. The wood frames so popular in Victorian times sometimes have a narrow gold inset, and this bright inner frame can greatly add to the finish of the completed picture. You can always get a replacement inset cut at a good frame shop if the old one has been damaged.

Although large, plain or polished wooden frames will cut down easily, gilt ones present a very much more complicated problem. This is because, under the gold, the wood in plain frames will have been faced with gesso and, in the case of the decorated Barbizon frames, with thick plaster compound or even papier mâché. These top layers will crack or break away when a saw is used on them. The corners of the new small frames may, therefore, need extensive repairs involving plastic padding and so much retouching of the gold that a complete regilding will be necessary — it being almost impossible to match the original gilding with modern equivalents.

The work of cutting down a large frame can easily be undertaken at home if you have the proper tools and equipment: a good-quality mitre box and stop block, a tenon saw, a mitre clamp or vice, a small drill and a hammer. Alternatively, a competent handy-man or carpenter may agree to do this work, and the small frame will be returned to you glued and pinned at the corners, so that you can do the finishing off at home.

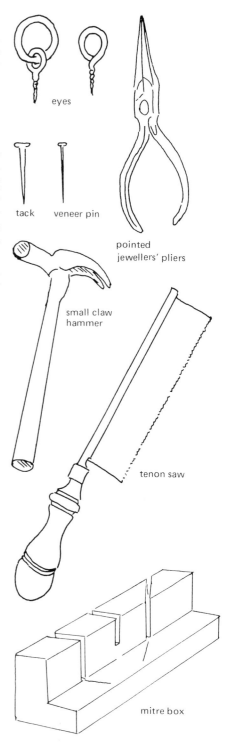

eyes

tack   veneer pin

pointed jewellers' pliers

small claw hammer

tenon saw

mitre box

Figure 18 Tools for making frames

29

This antique frame has been restored and polished. The flower design, featuring pansies, wild roses and primula, has been framed up using the free method, so that the well-padded back cushions the flowers against the glass.

REPAIR WORK

A good hardware shop will supply you with one of the modern compounds which you can use to build up a broken surface. The traditional creamy gesso mix of powdered chalk and glue size is, of course, excellent, but the new hard-drying compounds are quicker to use. Plastic padding or any similar material will serve very well, but make sure you buy the variety that can be sandpapered down when it has dried. Carefully clean away cracked, broken or loose pieces of old gesso around the place that needs a repair with a small brush. Apply the plastic padding according to the manufacturer's instructions, and use a small palette knife to build it up and make it smooth before it hardens. Finally leave it to dry completely, then rub it down with the finest grade of sandpaper (known as 'flourpaper').

Before embarking upon extensive repair work, you should be aware that it may be extremely difficult to match up colour. You may well find it easier to repaint an entire frame.

Gold frames

Matching up the shades of gold is seldom successful, so you should normally consider regilding the whole surface of the frame. First of all it must be sandpapered down to the original gesso, using first a fine sandpaper and finally flourpaper. Always rub with the grain of the wood so as to obtain a completely smooth finish. If it is necessary to fill cavities with gesso ground, you can manufacture your own by soaking a sheet (or granules) of rabbit skin glue in water overnight, then diluting it in water (15 parts of water to one of glue), and boiling in a double boiler until it is the consistency of gelatin. Mix this with whiting (chalk) to the consistency of cream, then apply it to the frame with a palette knife, and allow to dry. When completely dry, it may be sandpapered smooth.

Now it is possible to use the true gold leaf which will give a brilliant shining surface, but its application requires expertise and it is also very expensive. About 25 sheets of gold leaf, 8 cm (3¼ in.) square, are supplied together in one 'book'. First apply an adhesive layer of gold size (or thin warm glue with 20% methylated spirits added), leave it to dry until it is just tacky, and then apply the gold leaf. Lay a sheet of gold leaf out on a hard cushion, then with a sharp knife cut a piece a little larger than the size required. Pick it up by means of a flat brush which you have first charged with static electricity by drawing it across your hair, and place it on the frame, then press it down with a dry swab of cotton wool or a wooden block. Leave it to dry overnight, then finally rub it backwards and forwards with a burnisher to obtain a high lustre. This process is a skilled craft in its own right, and it requires expert tuition to achieve a professional result.

Remember that this extremely bright and true gold can overwhelm a pressed flower design by its very brightness, and it may well be that the softer 'antique' finished gold is to be preferred. Liquid gold paint (such as 'Liquid Leaf' in 'Classic' or 'Renaissance' gold) is excellent for this type of finish. It can be painted on, and the colour can be darkened further by the cautious addition of one of the earth pigments, such as umber or sienna. These can be bought at art shops in small tubes of oil paints (Raw Umber or Vandyke Brown are splendid for this purpose). 'Goldfinger' (manufactured by George Rowney & Co Ltd) can also be applied straight from the tube with a soft cloth.

When the repair work necessary is very small, a general touching-up of a frame may be all that is required. For this purpose an application of a gold wax polish (such as 'Treasure Gold Wax') can be excellent, and will bring back life to a slightly tarnished frame.

Figure 19 Lengths of moulding cut to size and mitred

Wooden frames

Plastic wood is the best material to use on this type of frame for it can be sandpapered, stained or varnished easily, and is simple to work with. Make sure that the cracks at all the corners are filled.

Some old frames which are badly scratched and stained will take on a new lease of life if they are cleaned, sandpapered smooth and then spray-painted. Beware of using sprays in the house, as the fine mist of paint is likely to overshoot the newspaper which you have laid on the table or carpet. A garage is the safest place for spraying frames.

FRAME MAKING

It will not be difficult to find a shop which stocks frame mouldings. The main problem will be to choose one or two out of the seeming myriad samples that are offered to you. At first, choose the simplest style and colour; as you gain in experience you may become more adventurous. If you do not wish to mitre your own lengths, you may ask the shop assistant to supply you with the short mitred lengths for a small extra charge. This will mean that all you have to do is to glue and pin the corners (figure 19). Pieces cut to internal measurements of 15 cm (6 in.), 17.5 cm (7 in.) or 20 cm (8 in.) will make up into useful sized frames. If you intend to use moulding that is wider than 1.2 cm (½ in.) the use of mitre clamps is essential.

Making a frame with wide moulding

There are two sorts of mitre clamps which can be used: neither is expensive and both are simple to use. The first type of mitre clamp is made of metal, and will only secure one corner at a time (figure 20). The clamp can be screwed down to a work bench, and the holding wedge mechanism tightened by two screws — one against each length of moulding. The second consists of four triangular corner clamps (figures 21-3), each one with a pair of spring, swivelling wedges, which will hold two lengths of moulding in place

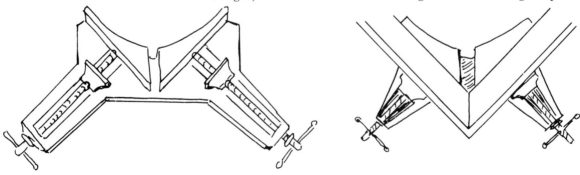

Figure 20   The corner of the frame inserted in the corner clamp

for gluing at an angle of 90° — providing the moulding does not exceed 4 cm (1½ in.) in width. The following instructions can be used equally well with either type of clamp.

1 Smooth and clean the ends of the moulding lengths.

2 Take one length and slide it into the left-hand channel of the corner clamp until it is 6 mm (¼ in.) out from the corner.

3 Put a thin layer of glue on the left end of the second length of moulding and slide it carefully into the right-hand channel of the same clamp until it is also 6 mm (¼ in.) from the corner.

4 Press the clamp corner against a firm surface and gently push the two pieces of moulding home into the right-angled corner where the glue will hold.

5 Wipe off any excess glue, being particularly careful not to leave any smears on the moulding surface, and make sure that the rebate is clear.

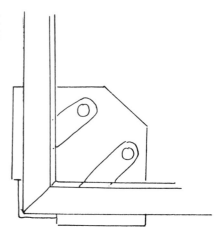

Figure 21 The mitre clamp holding the frame with the springs fixed in the rebate

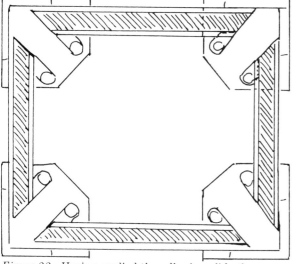

Figure 22 Having applied the adhesive, slide the moulding smoothly into the clamps to join the corners

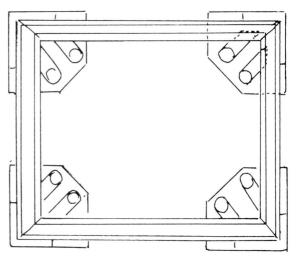

Figure 23 The moulding held tight by the springs in the mitre clamps

6 Repeat this process with the other three corners. Extra care must be taken with the fourth corner, and the fourth piece of moulding will have to be glued at both ends.

7 Allow the frame to set and dry completely. Release it from the clamps.

8 Stand the frame upright, and nail small veneer pins across the corners.

9 Make sure that the heads of the veneer pins are not above the wood surface. If necessary, use a larger nail with a blunt point to countersink them. Fill and paint the holes with the correct colour paint.

Figure 24 Hammer a veneer pin through the corner

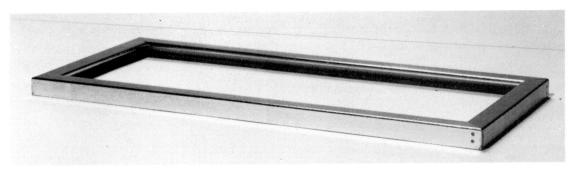

A simple rectangular frame made from 1.5 cm (⁵⁄₈ in) gold-leaf moulding. The corners are mitred, glued and pinned on one side only. The indentations left by the recessed veneer pins have been filled, and require a final touch of gold paint.

Making a frame with narrow moulding

1 Lay old newspapers on a table to protect the surface of the table and to provide a grid on which to base the right angles, along the columns of print (figure 25).

2 Smooth and clean the angled edges of the framing lengths.

3 Apply glue thinly to one end of one length. Lay it on the newspaper along a line of type.

4 Glue the second length in a similar manner. Lay this one at right angles to the first, using a column of type on the newspaper to provide the right angle.

5 Press the corner together.

6 Glue the third and fourth lengths and join them together at the respective corners, keeping the angles at 90°, and the lengths lying either along the lines of type or down the columns.

7 Put a running noose in a length of string, slip it around the outside of the frame and pull it tight. Secure it with a knot.

8 Clean off the excess glue and leave the frame to dry flat.

9 When quite dry, take off the string, stand the frame on one side, and hammer small veneer pins across each corner. Fill the holes if necessary, and paint.

The obvious advantage of undertaking this framing yourself is that you can experiment with different types of moulding easily, and the cost of the completed frame will be less than having it made any other way. There are of course many excellent small firms who will make up frames for you,

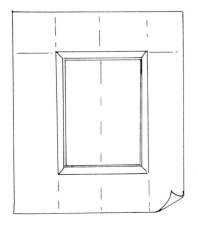

Figure 25 The lines of print on a newspaper will help give 90° angles

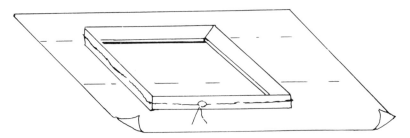

Figure 26 Hold the glued corners together with a strong noose, using a slip knot, and tighten firmly

and if you are prepared to order a number of similar-sized frames, you should be quoted very competitive prices. A minimum order might be in the region of two dozen frames, all in the same moulding but with some variation in size, and the price should include both glass and backing, the latter being either of cardboard or of hardboard.

READY-MADE FRAMES

A wide variety of ready-made frames can be bought from shops. The sales assistants in frame-making shops are specialists dealing exclusively in all types of frames and mouldings, and will give you expert advice about the subject. Most large departmental stores and photographic shops also stock picture frames, but these will usually be the smaller types.

Gold-leaf frames of fine quality wood are often imported from countries such as Italy, and they can be bought in a wide range of sizes starting from 5.5 cm (2¼ in.) across. They are excellent for flower pictures but are expensive. Avoid buying the cheap plastic copies; the 'gold' will scratch off and the backing cannot be secured firmly enough. Always be very careful before you buy cheap frames: mouldings made of metal, plastic compounds and cheap hardwood are very unsatisfactory to use. Pressed flowers must be framed up tightly against the glass, and any method other than the well-established one of firmly embedding veneer pins will probably cause disappointment.

The very diminutive frames are a little difficult to handle, so the beginner should first gain experience using frames about 15 cm (6 in.), 17.5 cm (7 in.) and 20 cm (8 in.) in height before progressing to the miniature and the large scale ones. Deep frames with convex glass are expensive, and not suitable for framing pressed flowers.

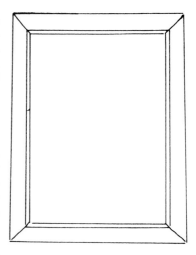

Figure 27   The completed frame

GLASS

Standard picture glass can be cut to any size at any glass shop; curved shapes are a little more expensive. The most suitable thickness is about 2 mm ($^3/_{32}$ in.). Non-reflecting glass is of no particular advantage in flower pictures. Always make sure that the glass fits well into the rebate of the frame.

Old pictures bought in antique shops and at sales often have the original glass in them, and this can sometimes be very thin, needing extra care in handling. This very thin glass has a charm of its own, and despite the occasional imperfections is well worth using again.

When cutting glass at home, wear gloves, and handle it firmly. You will need a clean piece of material on which to lay the glass, a glass cutter (a special tool with a rotatable head giving several cutting wheels), a straight edge such as a metal rule, and a T square. Mark the size required carefully,

Daisy shapes are used in this pair of Italian gilt frames. Cream, white, grey and green flowers and leaves contrast well with the dark green satin backgrounds. In the foreground are *Xeranthemum* and *Anthemis cupaniana*; the common daisy and mugwort are in the background. White and green hydrangeas, some

with centres of cow parsley, give solidarity to the arrangement.
Curved *Polygonum baldschuanicum*, Russian vine sprays, exochorda, and leaves
of anthemis, willow and fern, are used round the edges.

use the T square to ensure that the metal rule is lying across the glass at a 90° angle to the edge, then score along the surface from edge to edge of the sheet of glass, making one clean movement, and using the metal rule as a guide. Maintain an even downward pressure, and ensure that you have incised the line from start to finish, from edge to edge. Slide the metal rule under the glass, aligning it on one side of the line, and press down with your hand on the other side of the line. The glass should snap cleanly. Glasscutting requires expertise, and those without the proper facilities at home should ask the local glass merchant to cut the glass to size when buying it.

BACKING

Frames can be backed by strong cardboard or thin hardboard — both are equally good — with a final covering of art paper. It is also satisfactory to use a gummed paper strip around the edge of the frame. A guillotine (paper cutter) can be invaluable for cutting the cardboard and art paper, but a craft knife and a metal rule are also suitable. You will have to cut the hardboard with a small saw.

CARD MOUNTS

A mount forms an attractive addition to a pressed flower picture. Mounts are made of strong card with a matt surface that can be of any colour. They are used as a border within **the main frame to enhance the centre subject (page 39).** The range of colours is very wide — the soft, subtle colours being particularly good. Mount card is thick and can be cut at an angle, and the bevel of the aperture can be line-decorated in gold or coloured inks to give a finishing touch. It is possible to do this yourself but it is difficult to achieve a professional result, and it is therefore safer to order a mount through a good frame maker, or buy one from a stationer's or art shop. Ready-cut mounts are available in a range of sizes.

There is always a tendency for picture mounts to follow a fashion. The Victorians enjoyed gold ones, and in the 1930s wide cream ones were popular, while since the 1940s there has been an ever-growing tendency to have bright colours. This can be very effective; given a strong positive subject to be framed, the accentuation of one particular colour by the mount can be dramatic. Beware the picture where the mount and frame are in such dominance that you hardly notice the subject. Pressed flower pictures are, on the whole, a gentle and delicate breed and are easily overpowered by heavy framing, so be careful of the bright, flashy mount, and keep it narrow and soft coloured.

The shape of the cut-out in which the flowers are to be placed must, of course, depend on the frame. A rectangular

frame will happily take a rectangular, oval or round shape, while the oval frame will normally only take a cut-out of a similar shape. A rare but delightful find is the antique frame with a black or black and gold border painted on the glass itself. Flowers will look most attractive in one of these.

STORING FRAMES

Old frames bought at sales are often heavy to handle and bulky to store, and since you are probably only interested in keeping the frame, it is advisable to remove the picture. Remove the old wire and metal eyes, strip off the old backing paper, extract the nails with a pair of pliers and then you will be able to take out the backing and the picture itself. Clean the glass and frame thoroughly and store them separately. The frame is now light and easy to store, and you will be able to try it for size easily when you are planning a picture. The glass should be stored flat and wrapped in thick old

A 20 cm (8 in) square frame made from 13mm (½ in) black and gold moulding, glass, grey card mount, and hardboard backing have been cut to size and are ready for assembly. The flower design, set onto the paper or fabric backing, will be calculated to fill the space left by the aperture in the mount, and will be sandwiched between the mount and the hardboard.

This arrangement in shades of cream and white on a brown satin background is enhanced by a sage green mount, and set in a modern, unpolished wood frame with a gold inset. The flowers include snowdrop, polygonum, mayweed, yarrow, elderflower buds and berberis.

cloth or corrugated cardboard. Never throw away pieces of glass of a reasonable size; they can be cut down and used for smaller pictures. Always store frames carefully, away from excessive heat or damp, and protect their surfaces from being scratched.

Backgrounds in paper
and card

CHOICE OF BACKGROUND

One of the reasons why municipal flower beds often look so unreal and out of place is because they emerge from an asphalt background, and asphalt is about as far removed from nature as you can go. The impeccable ranks of red salvias and blue lobelias look far more pleasing in the parks where they are bordered by green grass. It is perfectly possible to mount natural dried flowers onto a square of shiny plastic sheeting, and no doubt, if you did this, it would achieve the same visual assault as the dusty paving stones do with the city flowers. This is an overdrawn example of what not to do, but your eye must be encouraged to understand this factor of harmony between subject and background and to acquire critical judgment. Often a background gives a key to the balance of colour in the picture as a whole; sometimes it does little more than highlight the shapes and profiles; but it should always be chosen, along with the flowers and the frame, as an integral part of the expression of an idea that is in your mind.

Perhaps the ultimate in background contrast was achieved in the now disregarded art of the silhouette. The inky black profile thrown into astonishing prominence by the dazzle of the unalloyed white ground was so effective that a depth of appreciation of the subject in the round was achieved. Arthur Rackham's enchanting silhouette illustrations are just as successful as the black decorations on Etruscan vases; line and shape is everything. You will find exactly the same sort of visual pleasure if you mount a pressed end curl of Virginia creeper onto a cream card: the sharpness of the three pointed leaves diminishing in size along a curve of stem, the whole enlivened by dark tendrils, will achieve a new beauty.

The final point to examine is that of colour, and the shade of the background may well be the base from which to start choosing the flowers: a soft cream backdrop to a design of blue flowers and dark foliage, leading the eye to a focal point of cream roses, perhaps, or a wide expanse of scarlet to hold a swag of harvest grasses for a picture to be hung on a grey painted wall. With these colourful ideas in mind the background cannot be dismissed as unimportant.

PAPER

Paper is the cheapest form of background, and the governing factor really lies in its thickness rather than its cost. You must have substantial 'body' in a paper to be able to cut and frame it up successfully. Ordinary writing paper, bank (flimsy typing) paper and any sort of lining paper will be too thin; good-quality drawing paper or coloured art paper will be much more satisfactory. Even the humble sugar (school drawing) paper will suffice. These thick papers, white, black and coloured, can be bought at art and craft shops and good stationers. White blotting paper itself can make a satisfactory background material. On the whole, smooth finished papers are more effective than rough ones; in fact, fabrics such as coarse-weave cottons and linens are often better than any rough-surfaced paper in that they are softer and more interesting visually. However, the main reason for using paper rather than fabric in a picture is that firstly it is cheaper and secondly it is simpler to use when you are starting. But if for artistic effect you are seeking a pure surface colour rather than colour broken by weave, then use paper or card.

The list of papers and cards given here is arranged in ascending order of cost. No reference can be reliably made as to the exact price because all prices tend to rise steadily and often vary from shop to shop. The cheapest sugar paper can still be bought at a very reasonable price, while the most expensive paper listed here is about nine times more.

Sugar paper

This is not available in a very wide range of colours, but the pale grey and the fawn are very good; the standard size is approximately 50 cm x 62.5 cm (20 in. x 25 in.), with a matt finish.

Art cover paper

This has an adequate range of colours, but some are too bright and harsh for the purpose of making pictures. White will be useful, for the surface is smooth and has a slight sheen. It is available in the standard size.

Cartridge or drawing paper

This is sold in blocks, books or standard-sized sheets, usually in white only, but colours are obtainable.

Art paper

This is available in black and some useful colours, with a smooth semi-sheen surface. It comes in the standard size.

Ingres paper

This is so called because this type of paper was favoured by the artist of that name. It is a soft coloured, gently flecked matt paper, and the grey, soft brown and fawn are very attractive. It comes in sheets considerably smaller than the usual standard size.

Canford cover paper

This paper has a surface similar to the art cover but the range of colours is much better. Chocolate, grey, fawn and white would all be very useful. The size is standard.

Art paper from France

There is an excellent type of paper which sells under the name of 'Mi-Tientes Canson'; it is by far the most expensive in this list. It is made purely from rags and so has a fine smooth finish and good colours. This is available only in metric sizing, and is a little smaller than the standard size.

CARD

Card is used as a background and base for making all different types of flower cards; these can be used as greetings cards for Christmas, anniversaries, birthdays and other occasions. It can also be used as a background material in flower pictures. There are a number of suitable types of white card on the market; there are not so many coloured cards, unfortunately, but they are worth hunting for. Most card is excellent for mounting flowers, from the cheap duplicating (reproduction stock) card to the good-quality art card (illustration board).

One of the advantages of paper and card over fabric is that it is possible to make the addition of an inked border, and this gold or black inner border, closely surrounding the flower arrangement, can be very attractive indeed. But whereas it is relatively simple to draw a border on a flower card that can be trimmed easily if any correction is necessary, it is much more difficult to ink with complete accuracy a border that has to go inside a frame. The least mistake in measurement, and the border lines will not be parallel with the frame and so the whole thing will have to be discarded. Circular borders are very much easier in this respect. Always ink in the border before any flowers are stuck down.

Card varies a great deal in surface finish, and if you wish to add a drawn border, it is advisable to test it for absorbency to ink from a pen before buying very much of it. Some card will soak up the ink, and the drawn line will spread out into the fibres as if it were poor-quality blotting paper.

Duplicating card

This is a smooth-finish, strong card and very suitable for making pictures. It comes in white only, the sheets measure

32.5 cm x 20 cm (13 in. x 8 in.) and the cost is very reasonable. Like everything else it will be cheaper if you buy it in bulk; there is slight variation in quality, so shop around.

White 'Egdon' card

This is a good sturdy card and is most suitable for backgrounds It comes in sheets 50 cm x 62.5 cm (20 in. x 25 in.) and is not expensive.

Ticket (display) board

Again this is a good strong, standard size card, but it is more expensive - about double the price of the 'Egdon'.

Unnamed card

You can buy unnamed card very easily from stationers and art shops. The price will probably be in the middle range and so will the quality. It is difficult to find coloured card, though blue and a rich red do sometimes appear on the retail market and these can be rewarding to use.

MAKING A GREETINGS CARD

Making a greetings card constitutes a simple introduction to the art of making pressed flower pictures, since the item is small, inexpensive, and quick to complete.

Materials

Card
Guillotine (paper cutter) or a sharp craft knife and a metal (or plastic but not wooden) ruler
Pencils, one H (very hard) and one 3 or 4 B (very soft)
Pen-holder and drawing nibs (nos. 3 to 5 will give variety in line)
Pair of compasses
Set square
Soft eraser
Black Indian ink, coloured inks, or gold water-based ink
Draughtsman's pen with a .5 nib (easy to use but expensive) or a fibre-tipped pen (a very good cheap alternative)
Latex-based adhesive (such as Copydex, UK, or resin-based, such as Elmer's Glue-All, USA)
Household scissors
Tweezers

Preparation

Measure the size of card carefully before you cut, and remember to allow double width for folding. Use the hard H pencil for marking and the guillotine for cutting. A hard ruler and a craft knife can be used, but never use scissors

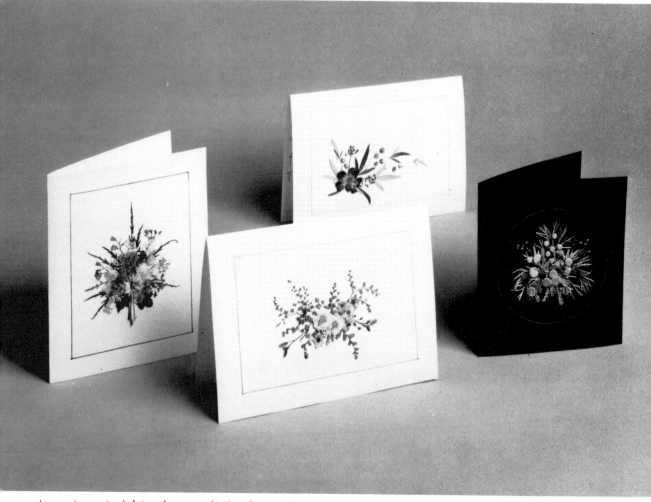

to cut a straight edge, as it is almost impossible to get a satisfactory straight line. Fold the card exactly in half after cutting, and press the fold quite flat.

When folding paper or card, fold in the direction of the grain to avoid a ragged or uneven fold. The direction of the grain can be seen in lightweight paper when it is held up to the light. To find the direction of grain in card, fold a test piece, or place a piece in water — the sides will curl up along the direction of the grain. When folding heavy card, score along the foldline first, along what will be the outer side, using a blunt tool and a ruler, and being careful not to break the fibres.

A card measuring about 14 cm x 10 cm (5½ in. x 4 in.) will be an easy size to start with; it is sensible to think of the size of your envelope before you start measuring out a card. Flower cards, being unframed, will benefit from an inked border drawn inside the edge of the card, either in black, gold or coloured ink.

Greetings cards can be made from white or coloured card, and the fold may be at the top or at the side.

With the H pencil and a ruler, mark the card with four light spots, one in each corner exactly 1.25 cm (½ in.) in from all the edges. With the pen, drawing nib and ink, and with the ruler turned the other way up, carefully draw lines joining the spots and making a border. *Draw slowly*. When using black or coloured ink, a calligraphy nib will be best (with a reservoir if possible), but when using gold ink, it will be much easier if you use an ordinary, old-fashioned writing nib. These do not have reservoirs, and are long and pointed. Take up only a little ink at one time, and draw the lines very slowly indeed.

You can vary the number and thickness of the lines in the border, for they will add a finish to the flowers on the card. One of the most attractive borders is a circular one. Place the card, preferably square in shape, open on a chopping board. Measure off the centre of the card and mark the spot with the pencil. Slide the pen into the compass and screw it in tight. Dip the nib into the ink, drain off the surplus, firmly press the point of the compass into the centre mark and through into the wood and turn the pen round slowly, keeping the compass tilted so that the nib is fairly flat. Black and coloured inks can be used most successfully this way; gold is very effective indeed, but it is difficult to use. For all pen and ink work, it is best to practise on scrap paper until you have mastered the technique. Always leave inked work to dry completely.

Making the design

When the card has been cut, inked, and dried, the flowers can be stuck lightly down with a latex-based adhesive. The one essential point about a flower card is that it should have a fresh and lively design which will catch the eye; set and studied designs are usually disappointing. The card is a transient thing, carrying good wishes and then finished with, simple in intent and simple in decoration. Experience gained on flower cards will be of great help to you when you start flower pictures.

As a beginner it will be hard to know where to start and which flowers to choose, so impose a discipline on yourself and use in your first design specimens from only three different species: for example, one type of leaf and two types of small flowers in your first card. In the second card, you can use one variety of leaf, perhaps, one type of seed head and one flower.

When gluing flowers to the card, never use thick blobs or smear the whole of the undersurface of the flower. Always use as little as possible. Wipe off excess or spilt glue at once, as excess glue will dry clear, but it will shine and be very noticeable.

CARD DESIGN 1

Equipment

A sheet of clean white blotting paper (to work on)
Small pair of eyebrow tweezers
Small pair of scissors
Latex-based adhesive
Cocktail stick or a sharpened matchstick
Small dish
Card (white duplicating), 11 cm x 15 cm (4½ in. x 6 in.)
Pen, ink (black) and ruler

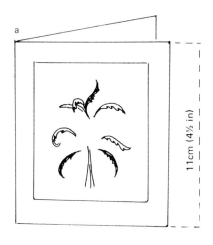

Flowers required

Small golden-brown bracken fronds
About eight open flowers and buds of anaphalis
Feathery reed heads (dark brown/black)
A few stalks

You will note that only three different materials are used here. Collect the old bracken and dry it off well. The fronds will curl as they dry, and these little curls can be broken off and pressed flat quite easily. The common reed grows fairly tall and is usually found in wet places. The darkness of the flowering heads depends on the length of time the flower has been out. A new spike is darker than an old one. The anaphalis flowers should not be pressed flat for this design, and the bracken needs only very short pressing. This design is not going to be placed under glass so the material can be allowed to stand out from the card surface.

Method

1 Fold the card in half and press flat. Draw a square border in black ink, and let it dry.

2 Put a little adhesive in the dish.

3 Take three well-shaped curls of bracken and, following the design in figure 28a, lay them loose on the card to get the triangle of the top and two base points adjusted in relation to the drawn border.

4 Pick the top curl up with tweezers, turn it over and, using the small stick dipped into the adhesive, touch it lightly at the bottom, the centre, and again at the top. Still holding the bracken in the tweezers, turn it back again and carefully replace it in its position on the card. Press down gently. Repeat with the two base curls of bracken. (The three shaded leaves in figure 28a illustrate this.)

5 Select another four bracken curls and lay them around the sides. Stick down. Break off any pieces that may extend into the centre of the design.

Figure 28 Greetings card design 1

47

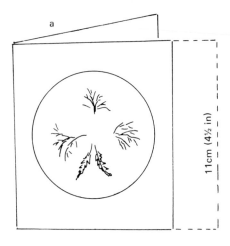

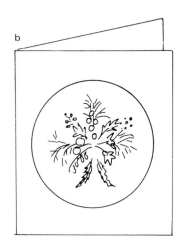

Figure 29 Greetings card design 2

6 Select a particularly curly piece of bracken, lay this just to the left of the top piece, let it curl up and away from the paper a little. Stick it down at the base only.

7 Select a few small pieces of cream and brown stalks. Cut them to the correct size and stick them down.

8 Disentangle about ten small pieces of reed and distribute them around the centre space between the bracken, using restraint (figure 28b). Stick with adhesive (a minute smear will be sufficient).

10 Add one small bud of anaphalis at the base of the top piece of bracken.

19 Lay anaphalis buds or profile flowers around the central space and stick down, using a single small touch of adhesive (figure 28c).

11 Add two or three very small bracken curls and a little reed if necessary and stick down.

12 Place one open, well-shaped anaphalis flower on the focal point and stick down.

CARD DESIGN 2

Equipment

As for Design 1, but using stiff black art paper 11 cm x 22 cm (4½ in. x 9 in.) and gold-coloured ink.

Flowers required

Silver grey foliage of two types: one feathery and one more solid (such as *Artemisia schmidtiana* and *Santolina chamaecyparissus*, or any silver foliage with delicate outlines)
Elderflower buds
Mimosa (wattle) buds and flowers
Traveller's joy buds or lime-tree buds
Polygonum

Method

1 Fold the card and press it flat. Draw a circular border in gold.

2 Lay three pieces of the delicate silver foliage in a triangle close to the gold circle as in figure 29a.

3 Stick them down with a light smear of adhesive, the top one first.

4 Add two small solid or spiky pieces of silver foliage at the base. Stick down.

5 Fix a small mimosa bud spray at top centre (figure 29b).

6 Add two elderflower bud clusters balancing on each side.

7 Place two further grey leaves, such as mugwort, over the stems of the elderflower buds.

3   Green and white flowers and leaves are set against a dark green background, set in
    an antique-look frame. The flowers include *Anthemis cupaniana*, xeranthemum,
    astrantia, cow parsley, hydrangea, snowdrop, anaphalis, and leaves of artemisia
    and Alpine alchemilla

4　The focal points of red-brown and yellow form pleasing
　colour contrasts to the green oval mount

5　The red satin background in a gold-leafed Italian
　frame adds warmth to the design

6　Daisies, anemones, polyanthus and forget-me-nots
　are given a light airiness by a soft blue background

7　A modern black and gold frame makes a dramatic effect
　teamed with pink and blue flowers on a purple
　silk background

The silver grey foliage in this card design shows up dramatically against the black background.

8 Add a small piece of polygonum.

9 Stick several dark buds of interesting shape on either side and on top of the feathery silver foliage.

10 Select two yellow sprigs of mimosa, place in towards the centre on either side and stick (figure 29c).

11 Add traveller's joy flowers and a little polygonum also around the centre.

12 Add the remaining mimosa flowers in the centre point itself, to give a brightness to the card.

CARD DESIGN 3

Equipment

As for Design 1, using white duplicating (reproduction stock) card 11 cm x 20 cm (4½ in. x 8 in.) and black ink.

Flowers required

Small dark green leaves of *Artemisia vulgaris* (mugwort) when reversed they are a silver grey
Polygonum baldschuanicum (Russian vine)
Calluna vulgaris, a mauve-pink heather (not an erica) which does not shed its leaves
White yarrow (milfoil)

Meadowsweet buds

Two white flowers of achillea or feverfew

Method

1 Fold the card in half and press flat.

2 Draw a square border round the card in black ink.

3 Place three of the smallest leaves of the mugwort dark side uppermost at the top of the design, and stick them down (figure 30a).

4 Add the two remaining larger leaves, and stick them down at the base.

5 Select six or seven pieces of *Polygonum baldschuanicum* (Russian vine), varying in shape, and place them around the design, leaving a space at the base. Stick down (figure 30b).

6 Place one spike of heather on the top leaf of mugwort and stick.

7 Select two small perfect sprays of meadowsweet, place them on either side of the heather and stick (figure 30c).

8 Choose about four pieces of heather and lay them around the centre space with a little yarrow to break up the mauve. Stick them all down.

9 Add three reversed mugwort leaves (silver) working inwards and stick.

10 Add a curve of meadowsweet buds in the centre. Stick.

11 Place the two white full-face flowers of achillea in the centre, one a little higher than the other and slightly overlapping.

12 Allow one of the heather stems to protrude below the design in the centre.

PREPARING A PAPER BACKGROUND FOR A
FRAMED PICTURE

Equipment

Card or paper
Finished frame
Glass cut accurately to fit the frame
Guillotine (paper cutter) or a craft knife and metal (or plastic) ruler
Pencils, one H (very hard) and one B (very soft)
Pen-holder and drawing nibs (nos. 3 to 5)
Pair of compasses
Set square
Soft eraser
Black Indian ink, coloured inks or gold water-based ink
Draughtsman's pen with a .5 nib or a felt-tipped pen
Latex-based adhesive   Household scissors   Tweezers

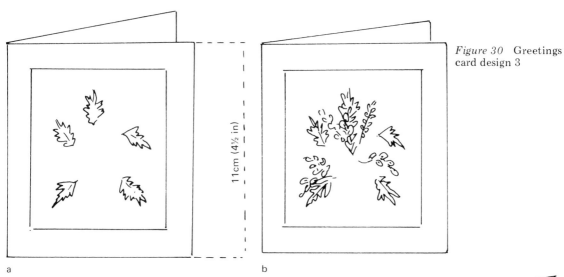

Figure 30 Greetings card design 3

a

b

c

Choice of background

Remember that using expensive paper and card for a background is a worthwhile investment. Cheap paper will look shoddy quickly, but good cartridge (drawing) paper will last as well in a flower picture as it does in an artist's sketch. The appearance of quality will be retained over the years. The background may be glossy or matt depending on the type of frame used.

Method

Clean the glass and the frame. Cut a shape from the paper or card a little larger than the outside frame measurement, and decide which side of the card or paper you wish to use as they often vary in sheen. Place the glass on the paper and, using the sharp H pencil, draw accurately round the outside of the glass, then remove the glass.

Using a ruler, measure and mark off the position of the border you wish to draw within the pencilled shape. When drawing a rectangular border, accurately mark four corner dots and join them up with pen and ink. When drawing a circular border, first measure and mark the centre point of the pencilled shape, place the compass point on this mark, and draw the circle round it. For an oval border, buy a commercial template from a stationer's or art shop, as it is too difficult to draw an oval shape accurately freehand.

Fabric backgrounds

CHOICE OF FABRIC

Your choice of fabric for a background will be influenced by three things. Firstly the cost, secondly your own preference in the matter of texture and sheen, and lastly the size and number of pictures you intend making. Cost is the most important factor, and if you plan a dozen pictures for Christmas presents, then you may well decide to buy a few metres (yards) of furnishing dupion rather than pure silk. Both dress and furnishing departments will of course offer a wide variety of far less expensive materials, and you will find suitable backgrounds quite easily.

Whether you like the shiny materials in preference to the matt, or whether the homespun look of linen is more satisfying to your eye than the sheen of satin, it is finally your own sense of visual pleasure that will guide you in the selection of fabric. Take into account where the picture is going to be hung if you can, for what is suitable for the wall of a working kitchen is unlikely to complement the expensive wallpaper and velvet curtains of a lounge. The third factor is the type, size and number of frames; a luxury fabric in a plain, narrow wood frame will do justice to neither, and the money will be wasted. Take your frame with you when you are choosing fabric for the first time.

Only a small piece of fabric is required for each picture. Half a metre (yard) will go a long way with frames of a modest size, and as a general rule natural fabrics are more suitable than man-made ones. There seems to be comfortable harmony between the 'natural' flowers and the 'natural' fabrics which is hard to put into words.

Cotton and cotton mixtures

Fine cotton lawn to heavy calico, the range of woven cottons is immense, and this is extended by the mixing of cotton with man-made fibres. Steer clear of patterns and loose weaves, bright colours and black. Pale shades are best; the lack of sheen in cotton makes dark colours seem dead. Do not despise the cheap unbleached tailor's backings; the colour will be sympathetic to flowers. It is always worth looking in both dress and furnishing departments for suitable material, and you will probably find that the cotton sateens and poplins will be most useful to you.

Linens

These are excellent for sturdy, coarse-woven backgrounds, but it is often difficult to buy pure linen by the metre (yard) in soft colours, and you may have to purchase linen type or man-made-fibre linen copy instead. Avoid bright, unsuitable colours, and beware the very coarse, heavy thread type — it can overpower flowers unless they are very large and bright.

Lining materials

These are the cheaper materials that are used to line both curtains and clothes, and they are often very good indeed if you are looking for a background with a neutral tone and a low sheen. Cotton sateen lining is a possibility, but Milium, the aluminium-backed lining, is excellent. The deep gold, pale silver grey, dark and apple green colours in Milium are very good, and the cost is reasonable.

Dupion

As a cheap substitute for real silk, furnishing dupion is unbeatable, the pronounced 'slub' effect (rough knobbles) is most attractive and the range of colours is wide and good.

Silk

The finest fabrics of all are undoubtedly the silks. All sorts of pure silks can be used, ranging from those from Thailand and China to those manufactured in Switzerland, and Macclesfield in the UK. The list of exotic spun and woven treasures sounds like the inventory of a merchant from the Orient: Shantung, Wild Silk, Honan Pongee and Jap Silk. As the amount you need each time will probably be modest you should be able to sample all these luxuries.

Notice the slub in the weave of some silks, which is caused by an infinitesimal thickening in the silk thread that is allowed to occur in the spinning. The uneven finish is most effective in a background against flowers. Heavy Pongee is probably the ultimate in coarse woven slub; it is used mainly for coats and suits and is very beautiful, but very expensive. Thai Silk and Wild Silk are excellent for flower pictures, but they are usually about double the price of the Shantungs, Honan Pongees and Macclesfield Silks. Jap Silk, which is really thin and flimsy, is uncomfortably light to use. Beware also of very shiny silks.

Colours in all these silk fabrics are usually beautiful, the pale shades giving a luxurious feel to a whole picture, and the stronger colours, such as rich red or chocolate brown, a glowing emphasis.

Satin

Satins can be used on either side, but be careful of the sheen for in cheap satins it can be harsh and ugly, while in pure silk satin the bias may cause problems when making up the picture.

Velvet, velveteen, velour, felt and baize

These materials all have thick surfaces and can be used for backgrounds successfully, but they will tend to give a solid colour effect because they all have non-reflective surfaces. When these materials are pressed tightly up against the glass, there will inevitably be an area along the edge of the picture where the fibres will be crushed, and this will show. In good-quality velvet this is particularly noticeable, and short-pile cotton or Dralon velvet is the best to use for this reason.

COLOUR

One of the unfortunate developments in the textile industry today is that the traditional vegetable dyes are being used less and less. The time involved in producing them is great, and so the cost is high. The chemist is taking over, but sadly the shades are sometimes lacking in subtlety, and he has not yet resolved the difficult task of making them as proof against sun and water as their traditional counterparts. The old vegetable dyes stood up to the years better. The silks that come from the Far East are often still dyed in the same manner, and as you look along the rolls of silks in the shop, the colours are generally kinder and more pleasing to the eye than those on the racks of nylons, terylenes and rayons. This is an area of preference which probably interests only a perfectionist, but it is a factor in your choice.

Suitability of colours

Easy colours
white/oyster/light or dark cream
gold/coffee/chocolate brown
very pale soft greens/dark bottle green
very pale greys

Difficult colours
tomato red/ruby red
apple green
deep purple
black

Unsympathetic colours
most blues/turquoise/bright green
oranges/yellow
scarlet/pinks
metal threads

MAKING A FLOWER PICTURE USING THE FREE METHOD

There are two distinct techniques used for making flower pictures: the free method and the fixed method. Both are equally satisfactory when done well, and both require an equal amount of care, patience and experience to achieve success.

In the free method, the flowers and leaves are laid loose on the surface of a padded background base and are arranged carefully into the design you want, using the empty frame as a guide to the shape. When the design is completed, the glass is then lowered on top of it and the whole finally fixed into the frame. The pressure exerted between the glass and the fixed padded back alone holds the flowers in place.

The slow and totally absorbing occupation of arranging the flowers in the design that you have conceived is, of course, the same in both the free and fixed methods. The flowers and leaves laid upon the base are moved one way or the other while the design slowly evolves. You are free to experiment with different shades and shapes of flowers, or you can try a slight alteration in the focal point, but ultimately you will have created with your flowers a design of beauty which will satisfy your eye. Only when you have reached this point will the glass go down and you can safely leave it. Later you can return, alter and improve it to your heart's content.

When you are a beginner, be careful that you do not arrange, rearrange and alter the design again to the detriment of your original idea. Often the initial artistic concept may be lost in too much perfectionist manipulation. Disadvantages of this method are few, but beware the open door and the gusty wind before the glass is down for good; a jolt or a child rushing past can shift flowers. Replacing broken glass in a frame is usually impossible without having to rearrange the flowers, so sending a picture through the post is hazardous. Undoing a frame to capture a loose seed or to clean an overlooked smear on the glass requires the greatest care.

When incorporating a card mount into the picture, pad the backing fabric with a man-made fibre (such as Terylene) which has plenty of bounce, so that the flowers are cushioned through the cut-out hole right up against the glass. It is more advisable, however, to use the fixed technique when incorporating a mount.

Equipment

Frame   Glass to fit   Background fabric
Piece of hardboard the same size as the glass
Wadding (thin wadding is best or a thick one split in two)
Clear adhesive   Cutting-out scissors   Ruler
Felt- (fibre) tipped pen   Iron and a clean surface to work on

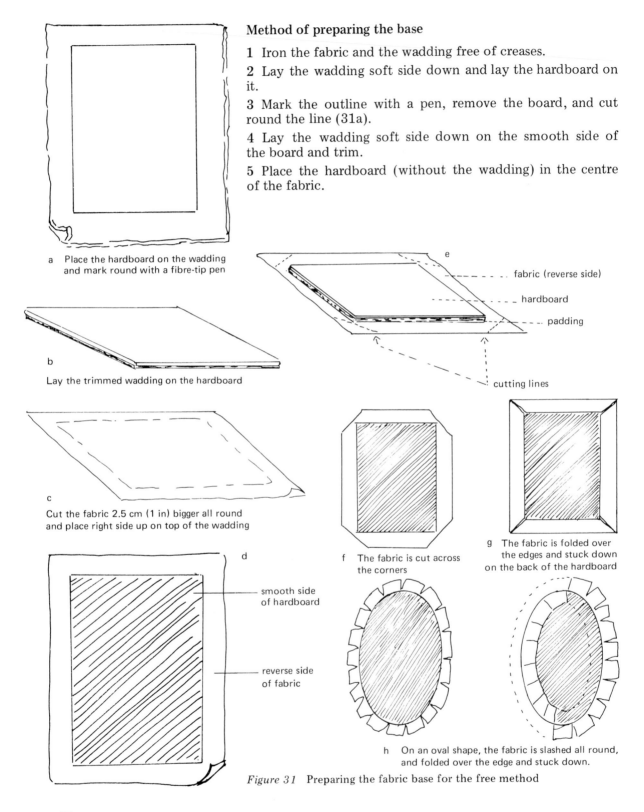

Method of preparing the base

1 Iron the fabric and the wadding free of creases.

2 Lay the wadding soft side down and lay the hardboard on it.

3 Mark the outline with a pen, remove the board, and cut round the line (31a).

4 Lay the wadding soft side down on the smooth side of the board and trim.

5 Place the hardboard (without the wadding) in the centre of the fabric.

a Place the hardboard on the wadding and mark round with a fibre-tip pen

b Lay the trimmed wadding on the hardboard

fabric (reverse side)

hardboard

padding

cutting lines

c Cut the fabric 2.5 cm (1 in) bigger all round and place right side up on top of the wadding

d

smooth side of hardboard

reverse side of fabric

f The fabric is cut across the corners

g The fabric is folded over the edges and stuck down on the back of the hardboard

h On an oval shape, the fabric is slashed all round, and folded over the edge and stuck down.

Figure 31 Preparing the fabric base for the free method

56

6 Align the edge of the board with the grain of the fabric. It is essential to get this correct. Use the selvedge or a drawn thread in rectangular shapes. The frame will be a useful check in rounded ones. Badly lined-up fabric will always show.

7 Mark an outline on the fabric at least 2.5 cm (1 in.) greater than the outside edge of the hardboard.

8 Remove the hardboard and cut out the fabric shape.

9 Place the wadding soft side down on the rough side of the hardboard (31b).

10 Cover with the fabric. Check the grain (31c).

11 Turn it over carefully, place it face down, and trim the material according to the shape of frame (31d to h).

12 Run a thin line of adhesive around the edge of the hardboard about 1.25 cm (½ in.) from the edge. (This should be the smooth side — it will not stick on the other.)

13 Lift the edges of the fabric and fold them carefully over the wadding and hardboard, and stick down. Start with the top and bottom edges to get the grain straight. Pull gently and evenly all round. The material must be stuck firmly so that the padded surface is taut, otherwise puckering will result when the glass is put on. If this happens, unstick one edge, pull tighter and re-stick. Thin gluing is best at all times.

14 The base is now ready for the flowers.

MAKING A FLOWER PICTURE USING THE FIXED METHOD

With this method, the flowers and leaves are laid loose onto a prepared background, the design is worked out, and after it has been perfected each specimen is lifted, lightly touched with an adhesive and replaced. Once the entire design has been fixed, the fabric can be safely lifted, the background cut down to the correct size, and the whole framed up.

The advantage of this method is that once you have experimented with and finally laid down the design outline in leaves and flowers, you can stick the fabric onto the background and continue to work upon the flowers leading gradually into the centre (or the focal point), without the risk of moving and changing the original concept. From a practical point of view it means that each stage can be stuck down once you are satisfied with the growth of the arrangement and that finally, when the whole picture is completed and fixed to the background, little can damage it. The minor repairs that are sometimes necessary after framing up are simple, and a back which becomes loose or a broken glass panel will not cause problems.

The main disadvantage is that once a flower has been stuck down it will be difficult to alter its position; dried

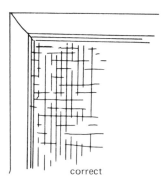

correct

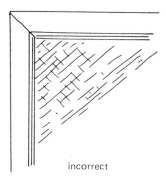

incorrect

Figure 32 The grain of the fabric must run vertically or horizontally

The design, made entirely of leaves, seed heads and flower buds, has been arranged and fixed on a background of pale green dupion fabric, and is ready for framing. The arrangement includes ferns, sorrels and grasses used with rose, jasmine, bramble and other leaves; small lupin leaves and buds of *Senecio cineraria* provide a focal point.

Figure 33 The frame is placed on the fabric, and the flowers are arranged loose in position; the flowers are then removed and pins are left to mark their positions

flowers are very brittle, and the adhesive nearly always leaves a mark on the fabric. Initially you may find you make mistakes, but you will find it very helpful if you use short pins as markers when the flowers have to be lifted (figure 33). If you work on a cork mat, the fine pins can be pushed in at an angle.

If a mount is to be used in the picture, the roughly cut background fabric can be stuck down onto the mount back with masking tape. This tape will peel off if necessary without tearing the card, and will be quite strong enough to hold the material in place.

Equipment

Frame
Glass to fit
Fabric

Iron-on backing (always match the weight of backing to the weight of fabric)

Cutting-out scissors
Pencil
Iron and a clean surface to work on

Method of preparing the base

1 Clean the glass.

2 Iron the fabric free of creases.

3 Lay the fabric face down, and place the glass on it.

4 Mark an outline with pencil at least 3.75 cm (1½ in.) greater than the outside edges of the glass.

5 Cut out – the grain of the fabric must run straight with the glass.

6 Cut a similar shape in the backing — a little smaller.

7 Place the fabric shape face down on the ironing board, put the backing with the (rougher) glue side down in the centre. Match up the grain of the threads.

8 Iron gently, using a warm iron.

9 Be careful to keep the grain of both materials in line as you iron.

10 Finish off with a cool iron on the right side. Too hot an iron may well result in the glue coming through the fabric and marking it. Be particularly careful with this when you are ironing very thin fabrics such as pure silks and satins. Guard too against stretching them; always iron in the direction of the threads and not across the bias.

Figure 34 When adding a card mount to the picture, pull the fabric taut across the aperture and fix it in position before arranging the design and framing up

Creating the design

Figure 35 Design faults to avoid

Not using the space properly

Overcrowding the picture

Placing the flowers too haphazardly

SHAPES AND SPACES

Look at the outline of the flowers laid on the background of a picture. The shape of the design fits like a jigsaw into the spaces of the background, but unlike a jigsaw the line between the two must be defined and not disguised. Outside the space of the background lies the frame, and it is the balance between the shape of the design and the shape of the frame that will be discussed in this chapter.

The periphery of the flower design must be apparent; a background and flowers of exactly the same colour will have no bite at all — the one will merge with the other. A colour or shade difference is essential to accentuate the outline. The second factor which will help to give the necessary definition is the line of the stems, while the third is the natural tilt of the flower heads in the arrangement leading to the focal point.

The mathematical permutations on the different shapes of frames, designs and foliage are colossal, and it would be impossible to describe more than a few of the combinations. However, it will help the beginner if a few basic designs can be drawn or worked out using well-known leaves, flowers and ferns.

Avoid the common mistakes illustrated in figure 35: not using the space to full advantage, overcrowding the picture, and placing the flowers haphazardly without form or line.

DESIGN 1: TRIANGULAR DESIGN IN A RECTANGULAR FRAME

Choose an off-white background colour. Put the clean frame over the prepared background fabric, have your store of leaves and ferns beside you, and the tweezers in your hand.

Stage 1

Always start by fixing the topmost point of the design. Lay a pointed, feathery-headed grass centrally in the picture about three-quarters of the way up — your eye will guide you to the correct height in relation to the frame.

Take two pieces of fern, one bending to the right and one to the left. Place them low down in the frame, one pointing

gently down into the right-hand bottom corner and the second piece pointing to the left-hand corner. Each fern should follow its natural curve, and each tip should be equidistant from the frame edge.

You have three points now. Your eye will begin to imagine a triangular shape around them, and the sides of this outline must now be defined. Take a small sage leaf and place it about half-way up the line on the right-hand side, the tip of the leaf pointing into the top right corner and set out a little from the line. Repeat with a small willow leaf on the left side of the design, but place this leaf slightly lower than the sage.

A busy little arrangement in shades of cream and green, set in a circular gold antique frame with a green background. The centre of the green *Hellebore foetidus* is accented with a floret of cow parsley; other flowers include *Anemone blanda*, mugwort, wild strawberry blossom, and leaves of *Chrysanthemum haradjanii* and silverweed.

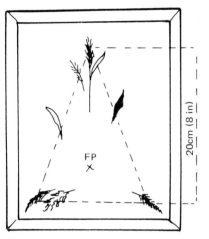

Figure 36 Triangular design in
a rectangular frame

You now have the basis of a triangular shape in the picture with the top defined by the grass point, the base by the two ferns, and the hard lines of the sides softened by the sage and willow. The darkened foliage in figure 36 illustrates this.

Stage 2

The top grass is a hard shape. Take a second, smaller piece of the same grass and place it beside the first (on the left side, a little lower down and leaning outwards to the left). Take a small willow leaf and lay that across the two grass stalks so that it leans slightly to the right and the tip of it **is just slightly above the tip of the second grass. The hard** top of the design has been altered; it has softened in shape and is interesting.

Consider the two ferns at the base of the design: that, too, is hard and uncompromising. Take a well-shaped leaf of artemisia and place it near the left-hand fern, pointing downwards, at an angle to the left. The line of the leaf will cut across the imagined hard line between the tips of the ferns. The outlined foliage in figure 36 illustrates this stage.

Focal point

Imagine that the five basic leaves had long stems continuing into the picture centre. The place where they would meet each other is the focal point (FP), and this is the point to which you must now work with your flowers. The natural tilt of the flower heads and their 'expression' should lead towards it, and the most dominant flower should ultimately be placed there.

Colour

Although you have been working at shape and structure, the colour factor must also go hand in hand. The background you have been working on is undemanding, and you will notice that the shades of the foliage have deepened in strength down the picture giving a weight to the design. The colour is graded from the pale grasses through sage and willow green to the darker and more definite olive green of the ferns.

Suggestions and instructions for filling in the centres of these designs will be discussed and illustrated in the next chapter.

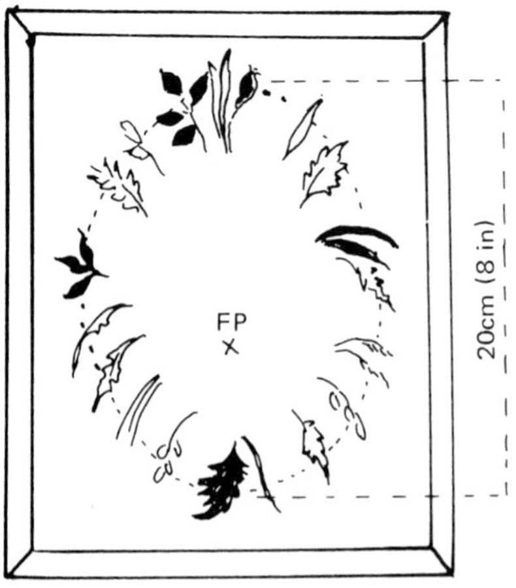

DESIGN 2: OVAL DESIGN IN A RECTANGULAR FRAME

1 Choose an off-white background. Place a perfect white rosebud at the top of the design and put a rose leaf beside it curving slightly to the left (figure 37).

2 A substantial leaf of silverweed (cinquefoil), laid with the reverse side uppermost, should lie at the bottom of the design, curving to the left.

3 Half-way down the right side and also curving, place a

Figure 37 Oval design in a
rectangular frame

small fork of willow leaves, and opposite it the balance can be held with a small *Clematis montana* leaf.

4 The four quarters can be brought into focus with the leaves of willow, sage, pyrethrum and anthemis, and the final addition of leaves and grasses will complete this oval outline which is a 'busy' one.

5 The focal point is low, unless the picture is to be hung in a very low position on a wall.

DESIGN 3: BROKEN RECTANGULAR DESIGN IN A RECTANGULAR FRAME

1 Choose a cream background. Place a red-brown 'Mermaid' rose leaf on the right side curving slightly upwards, half-way up the design (figure 38).

2 A warm brown bracken frond should lie half-way up on the left side to balance.

3 Take a sharply defined stinging nettle head with small leaves and flowers and place it with the stem curving upwards and left from the centre of the design. All three tips of foliage should be equidistant from the frame edges.

4 Two dark *Clematis montana* leaves are laid to droop down below the bracken, one of them reaching the imaginary line of the rectangle's base and the second just short of it.

5 A small piece of yellow bracken should be placed below the 'Mermaid' leaf on the right side, curving downwards.

6 The focal point in this design will be fractionally below centre.

DESIGN 4: DOUBLE CURVE DESIGN IN A RECTANGULAR FRAME

1 Using a pale cream background, take a curved fern, such as maidenhair, and lay it with the tip in the top right-hand corner, the stem curling down into the centre (figure 39).

2 A similarly curved leaf of anthemis should be laid in the bottom left-hand corner, the stem also bending up into the centre.

3 The point at which the two lines meet is the focal point, and the other leaves must appear to start from here. It will be seen from figure 39 that a rose leaf laid near the fern will spring the shape outwards and thicken it, while a twist of polygonum pressed before it is fully out will balance it below.

DESIGN 5: TRADITIONAL ROUND DESIGN WITH STEMS IN A RECTANGULAR FRAME

1 Choosing a pale cream background, lay a piece of well-shaped tamarisk at the top centre of the design (figure 40).

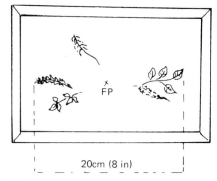

Figure 38 Broken rectangular design in a rectangular frame

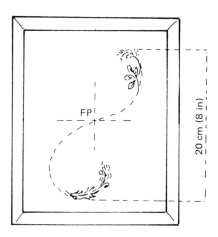

Figure 39 Double curve design in a rectangular frame

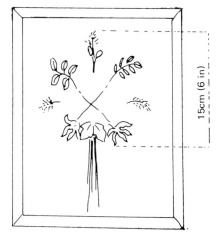

Figure 40 Traditional round design with stems in a rect-angular frame

63

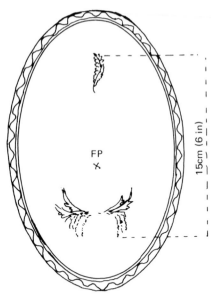

Figure 41 Triangular design in an oval frame

2 Lay several loose stalks centrally at the base. The top of the tamarisk should be a little further in from the top edge of the frame than the ends of the stalks are from the bottom frame edge.

3 The four strong points of this design lie on the diagonals.

4 Place a five-fingered passion flower leaf on the bottom right-hand diagonal, just up from the top of the stalks. A second similar leaf but reversed to give colour variety should be placed on the other side of the stalks.

5 Place a dark, curved jasmine leaf on the top right diagonal and a wild rose (dog rose) leaf on the top left.

6 Place two more pieces of tamarisk at right and left of the ring outline, both with a slight curve to them if possible.

7 Place two small, dark brown leaves of Virginia creeper at the top of the stalks, overlapping each other.

8 The top piece of tamarisk is too neutral. Take two dark buds of Japanese anemone and place them on top of it, letting one curve a little to the left and the second and lower one a little to the right.

DESIGN 6: TRIANGULAR DESIGN IN AN OVAL FRAME

1 Against a very pale green background a dark fern will give dramatic height to this shape. Choose one with a slight natural curve, or a straight one with a curly tip. Lay it centrally in the picture (figure 41).

2 Select some tassels of the stinging nettle flowers and some small leaves of the appropriate size. Set two cascades of these very dark green flowers on either side of where the fern stem would lie. The small leaves should spring out from the tops of the two flower clusters.

3 The focal point is low in this design.

DESIGN 7: FORMAL STAR DESIGN IN A ROUND FRAME

1 Choose an oyster background. Take three points of Japanese maple by breaking three equal-sized pieces of leaf off a big five-leaflet palmate leaf. Choose one with the tips curling just a little.

2 Place these equidistantly around the picture — make sure that the three tips are exactly the same distance from the frame edge (figure 42).

3 Take three pieces of silver foliage (santolina or a similar type with feathery small leaves in clusters) and intersperse the sharp red maple points with the softer grey ones. Set them back slightly from the imaginary circle shape.

4 The focal point lies in the centre where the stems meet.

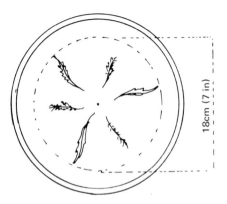

Figure 42 Formal star design in a round frame

Completing the design

COLOUR IN FLOWER PICTURES

Colour arouses more subjective feelings than almost anything else in the world of arts and crafts. An apparently simple shade combination will be enthusiastically praised by one person but be declared anathema by another. Reasons are seldom given — pleasure or distaste is usually instant and instinctive.

We, and the word embodies a splendid international conglomerate, are all as varied in our likes and dislikes as we are in age, sex and race. Governed by climate, persuaded by fashion and influenced by tradition, it is almost impossible to make wise statements to the effect that one colour goes with such a one, or that other colours will necessarily clash when they are in close proximity to each other. The only possible authority to quote is nature — certainly the most expert colour mixer of all time. We can look at the groupings of colours in the spectrum and assess the probability of certain colours blending happily together and in the end reach some sort of conclusions that we may apply to the making of flower pictures.

It might be helpful to look at the circle of the spectrum and recognize the primary colours and their groups. (The colour indigo has been omitted for simplification.) Red, blue and yellow are the primary colours and each one has its own family or shade group. For example, red mixed with blue gives violet and when it is mixed with yellow it will produce orange. The shade group of red is therefore as follows:

Red group

Violet — secondary colour

Red — primary colour

Orange — secondary colour

The remaining colours in the spectrum, that is, yellow (primary), green (secondary) and blue (primary), do not have any red in them at all.

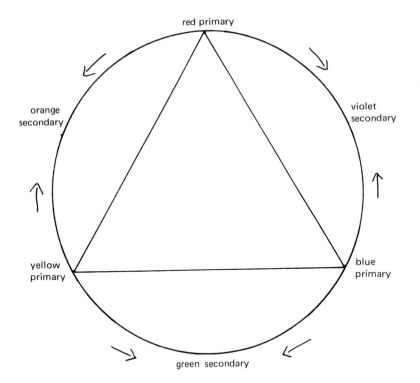

Yellow group

Orange — secondary

Yellow — primary

Green — secondary

(Colours without yellow
are red, violet, blue)

Blue group

Violet - secondary

Blue — primary

Green — secondary

(Colours without blue
are yellow, orange, red)

Figure 43 The colour spectrum

Look at the circle of colours in figure 43. Each of the two primaries, when paired together and with the intermediate secondary colour, will always be comfortable, so hesitate before you add to this combination any of the colours from the family group of the remaining primary. (This colour and its shade group lie, of course, exactly on the opposite side of the spectrum circle.) For example, red, violet and blue will blend happily, but the inclusion of orange, yellow or green will be uncomfortable. Translate this in terms of flowers: while red roses, mauve willow herb and blue lark-spur will mix together beautifully, they will not take happily to the addition of a cheerful yellow buttercup.

Following on from this it is easy to include in its own relative group any of the paler or darker tones of a colour. The tints or shades — it does not matter what you call them — of red, for example, will fall naturally into the red group. This may range from the pink of a hydrangea to the deep red of a wallflower. The intensity or neutrality of a colour will not essentially alter the rules that govern the colour grouping.

The one classic exception to this theorizing is the colour green in the foliage of plants. Whether this is because we live in a world where this colour is paramount and where nature has conditioned our eyes, or whether there is a purely scientific reason why the colour is more restful to the optic nerve, it is hard to tell, and it is probably both of these things. The fact remains, however, that green, in one shade or another, is universally comfortable with all flowers. Remember, though, that not every shade of green is compatible with all the others: a bright turquoise will be incompatible with a rich olive green, and green leaves must be matched up with the colours of the flowers in your design. Always treat a background of green with great care; it is not the exception here.

With these important conclusions in mind you can mix red and bright, bright pink together and know that in the East the Japanese have been doing this successfully for centuries in kimono silks and sleeve linings. Realize, too, that black backgrounds need not necessarily be funereal — it will depend upon which side of the world you happen to live, and with all this licence you can experiment to your heart's content. Somebody, somewhere in the world, will approve of the choice of colours you make.

Problem colours

1 Keep the picture small if you are using strong, bright colours in flowers, frames and background. A fuchsia has a beautiful and remarkable combination of colours, but too substantial an area of red, violet and pink can be daunting.

2 To have only harvest colours of fawns and creams, and fawns in flowers and background is dull. A total ensemble of this unrelieved neutrality can, in a picture as in clothes, earn itself the disagreeable title of 'varying shades of manure'! Give it a wholesome and generous pinch of either white or a dark colour. Remember that dark colours retreat and pale colours tend to advance in visual impact. A design with a complete imbalance of colour strength on the two sides, for example, may well give the bizarre effect that the whole thing is going to spin like a rotary drier!

3 Be cautious with orange: it is a strong vivid colour and usually needs toning down with browns or creams.

4 The acid colours, lemon yellow, 'bath-salts' pink and that evil, gangrenous green, are all disagreeable to other colours and difficult to use.

Colour suggestions

1 Harsh colours are softened by the addition of white or yellow. They are both excellent for persuading the rest of the colours to mix together.

2 Silvers, whites and creams can flourish when laid on a dark colour such as red, green or brown.

3 Dark colours can be extremely effective in a flower design and stand out best when contrasted with a pale background.

4 Pastel colours of all shades can be mixed together and will give the busy, gentle effect of an old patchwork quilt.

5 Match up a particularly strong colour in a room: a rich red, for example, can be echoed in the background with heavy flowers and a deep frame.

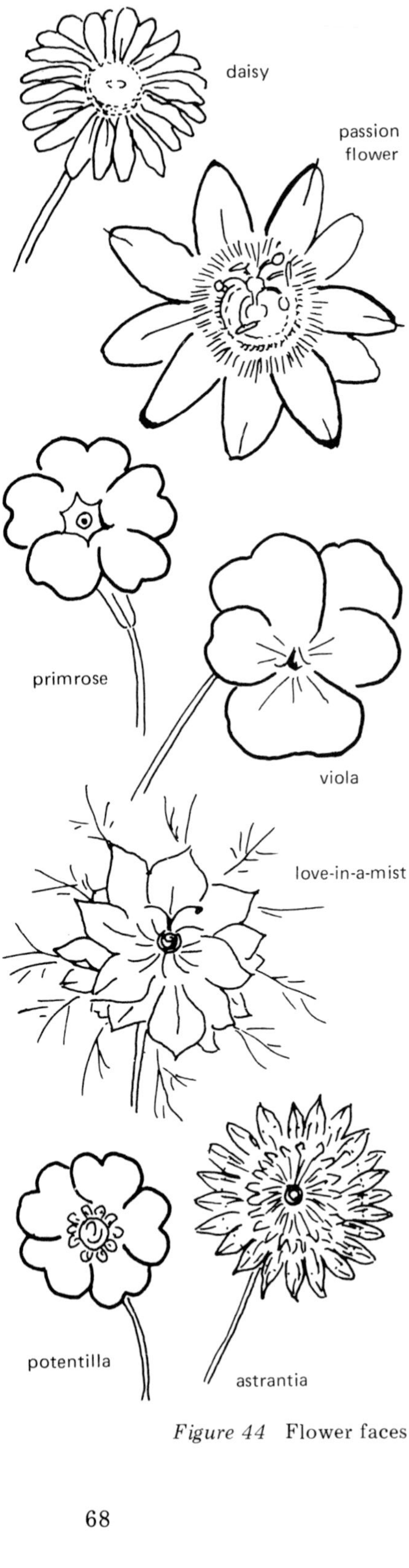

daisy

passion
flower

primrose

viola

love-in-a-mist

potentilla

astrantia

Figure 44 Flower faces

FILLING IN A DESIGN WITH COLOUR

The previous chapter described how to lay out the basic design, using foliage to define the outline. Now the central empty spaces in the design are to be filled in, using the colours and shapes of the flowers themselves, as a painter would his palette. Never attempt to place a flower upside down in a picture. Although you are not going to copy nature to the extent that you will allow yourself one rose to every 15 cm (6 in.) of stem for example, remember that a rose does usually have an upright stance. Similarly, flower heads that hang down on their stems in the garden can look very unnatural if they are placed in a picture gazing to the sky.

Strong contrasts in colours give a strong visual impact: a red rose laid beside white flowers, yellow mimosa (wattle) over brown leaves or bright blue hydrangea against cream hellebores — the list could be endless, but it should be kept in mind when you have laid down one flower and are wondering what to do next. Always build the shape in towards the centre of the picture, the focal point, and place the most important flower here where it will dominate the design both in its colour and shape. The faces of flowers have delightfully individual characters and this, too, will strongly affect the completed picture. The starry shape of a passion flower or the bright eye of a buttercup are completely different from the rather pensive expression of a pansy. Modesty is always associated with downcast eyes and averted face. Geums and fuchsias, cowslips and lilies all have this effect in a picture, and indeed the drooping flowers will give a considerably more muted effect than if there were big, bold daisies gazing out at you.

Colour should be repeated at various points in a picture. One particular shade set to one side can be repeated successfully on the opposite side, and this not only balances that individual colour strength in your design but will also give an extra line of definition across it. Dark colours give emphasis, and on the whole should be placed low down or centrally in a picture, but they will only produce this effect if they are highlighted by paler colours.

In the following pages there will be separate instructions for completing each of the seven designs outlined in the previous chapter. Each section will include a general list of suggested flowers necessary to complete the design artistically, and this will be followed up with a detailed list of the flowers as used in the pictures. There are three figures illustrating each design: the first, which was explained and illustrated in the last chapter, shows the initial outlining of the basic shape; the second, which is a purely diagramatic plan, will show the placing of the flowers, buds and extra leaves; while the third in each group will show the completed picture.

Simple wild and garden flowers are suggested for this seven-part exercise, but it may well be that the beginner will find it difficult to produce all the varieties from the press. For this reason the colour and approximate size of the chosen flowers have been given, so that it will be relatively simple to replace one variety with another. The number preceding each flower in the list will refer to its relative position as shown in the figure. The flowers will generally be added in a concentric pattern, always working inwards to the centre or focal point. Be careful not to overlap and partly hide the centres of flowers for they will lose their charm and appear 'blind' if this happens.

Trims, which are referred to throughout the designs, are small additions of material already used in making up the arrangement employed to finish and balance the design. It is impossible to specify all these extra pieces; your own eye will judge what is needed, but if in doubt, leave them out.

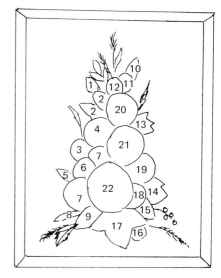

DESIGN 1: TRIANGULAR DESIGN IN A RECTANGULAR FRAME

Colours

Brown, yellow, cream, blue and white against an off-white background.

Flowers and foliage

1 Rosebud — cream, 1.25 cm (½ in.)
2 Sage leaf — grey, 2.5 cm (1 in.)
3 Daisy — white, 1.25 cm (½ in.)
4 Primula — dark brown, 2 cm (¾ in.)
5 Herb Robert leaf — red/green, 2 cm (¾ in.)
6 Hydrangea — blue, 2 cm (¾ in.)
7 Auricula — yellow, 0.5 cm (¼ in.)
8 Lady's bedstraw — black
9 Maple leaf — red, 3.75 cm 1½ in.)
10 Lavender — blue, 0.5 cm (¼ in.)
11 Daisy — white, 1.25 cm (½ in.)
12 Primula — yellow, 2 cm (¾ in.)
13 Maple leaf - - red/green, 2.5 cm (1 in.)
14 *Clematis montana* leaf — grey/green
15 Maple leaf — red
16 Primula — dark, 1.25 cm (½ in.)
17 Ivy leaf — 4.5 cm (1¾ in.)
18 Primrose — yellow, 1.25 cm (½ in.)
19 Small narcissus — yellow, 2 cm (¾ in.)
20 Single wild rose (dog rose) — cream, 3 cm (1¼ in.)
21 Pansy — brown, 3.75 cm (1½ in.)
22 Anthemis — yellow, 3.75 cm (1½ in.)

Trims

Dark elderflower buds and tiny mimosa (wattle) sprigs; use sparingly.

Figure 45 Filling in design 1

DESIGN 2: OVAL DESIGN IN A RECTANGULAR FRAME

Colours

Orange, brown, cream, white and a touch of yellow against an off-white background.

Flowers and foliage

1 Tagetes — orange, 1.25 cm (½ in.)
2 Wallflower — yellow, 1.25 cm (½ in.)
3 Ivy leaves — dark green, 2.5 cm (1 in.)
4 Primula — yellow, or brown, 2.5 cm (1 in.)
5 Hellebore, or single rose — cream, 3.75-5 cm (1¼-2 in.)
6 Anthemis — white, 5 cm (2 in.) and 3.75 cm (1½ in.)

DESIGN 3: BROKEN RECTANGULAR DESIGN IN A RECTANGULAR FRAME

Colours

Yellow, cream and blue against a very pale cream background.

Flowers and foliage

1 Caryopteris — blue, 1.25 cm (½ in.)
2 Silverweed leaf — reverse side uppermost
3 Buttercup (reversed) — yellow, 1.25 cm (½ in.)
4 Buttercup (full face) — yellow, 2 cm (¾ in.)
5 Three small hydrangeas — blue, 0.5-1.25 cm (¼-½ in.)
6 Cluster of elderflowers — cream, 2.5 cm (1 in.)
7 Elderflowers in buds — dark brown
8 Buttercup — yellow, 2.5 cm (1 in.)
9 Two achillea florets — white, 0.5 cm (¼ in.)
10 Three lobelia flowers — blue
11 Mimosa sprig — yellow, 3.75 cm (1½ in.)
12 Daisy — white, 2 cm (5/8 in.)
13 Wild rose — cream, 2.5 cm (1 in.)
14 Wild rose — cream, 2.5 cm (1 in.)

Figure 46 above Filling in design 2
Figure 47 below Filling in design 3

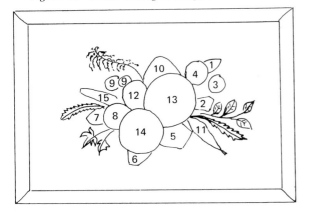

15 Mimosa sprig — yellow, 2.5 cm (1 in.)

Trims

No trims should be necessary; this is a simple design.

DESIGN 4: DOUBLE CURVE DESIGN IN A RECTANGULAR FRAME

Colours

Pink, blue, purple and a touch of white against a pale cream background.

Flowers and foliage

 1 Silver leaf
 2 Hydrangea — blue, 1.25 cm (½ in.)
 3 Purple geranium — purple, 2.5 cm (1 in.)
 4 *Clematis montana* leaves — dark grey-green
 5 Maple leaf — dark red
 6 Senecio leaf — silver
 7 *Clematis montana* leaves — reversed
 8 Astrantia — green, 2 cm (¾ in.)
 9 Hydrangea — blue, 1.25 cm (½ in.)
10 Artemisia leaf — small, grey
11 Anthemis leaf — small, grey
12 Hydrangea — pink, 1.25 cm (½ in.)
13 Purple geranium — purple, 2.5 cm (1 in.)
14 American Pillar rose — pink, 4.5 cm (1¾ in.)

Trims

Trim with two tendrils and Queen Anne's lace (cow parsley/chervil).

DESIGN 5: TRADITIONAL ROUND DESIGN WITH STEMS IN A RECTANGULAR FRAME

Colours

Red, cream, white and pink against a pale cream background.

Flowers and foliage

 1 Cluster of Queen Anne's lace — white, 2.5 cm (1 in.)
 2 Two or three florets of may — pink, 0.5-1.25 cm (¼-½ in.)
 3 Reversed miniature rose — red, 2.5 cm (1 in.)
 4 Cluster of elderflowers — cream, 2.5 cm (1 in.)
 5 Three or four achillea florets — white, 1.25 cm (½ in.)
 6 Cluster of Queen Anne's lace — white, 1.25 cm (½ in.)
 7 Fuchsia — red, 2 cm (¾ in.)
 8 Two fuchsia buds — red, 0.5 cm (¼ in.)
 9 Rosebud — pink, 0.5 cm (¼ in.)
10 Three achillea florets — white, 0.5 cm (¼ in.)

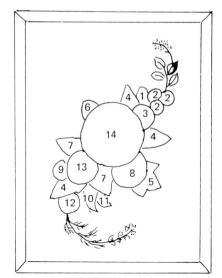

Figure 48 Filling in design 4

Figure 49 Filling in design 5

11 Rosebud — red, 1.25 cm (½ in.)
12 Common daisy — white, 2.5 cm (1 in.)
13 Rose — red, 3.75 cm (1½ in.)
14 Wild rose — cream, 3.75 cm (1½ in.)
15 Wild rose — cream, 3.75 cm (1½ in.)

Trims

Japanese anemone buds, elderflower buds and five or six loose stems. Use trims sparingly in this design. Use stems of slightly differing thickness, and try to get a gentle outward curve in two of them at the base. Place a small leaf where the stems join the design, or tuck the ends well out of sight.

DESIGN 6: TRIANGULAR DESIGN IN AN OVAL FRAME

Colours

Pink, white, mauve, red and blue against a very pale green background.

Flowers and foliage

1 Willow leaf and three onion florets or chives — pink, 1 cm (³⁄₈ in.)
2 Sprigs of rush — brown, small
3 Heather — mauve, 3.75 cm (1½ in.)
4 Clusters of heuchera — dark red

Figure 50 Filling in design 6

5 Clusters of helianthemum buds — grey green
6 Ivy leaf
7 Two or three lobelia flowers — bright blue
8 Sprigs of rush
9 Willow-herb — pink/purple, 1.25 cm (½ in.)
10 Senecio leaf — silver
11 Achillea — white, 1.25 cm (½ in.)
12 Willow-herb — pink, 1.25 cm (½ in.)
13 Willow-herb — pink, 1.25 cm (½ in.)
14 Daisy — white, 1.25 cm (½ in.)
15 Viola — purple/white, 0.5 cm (¼ in.)
16 Viola — purple/white, 2 cm (¾ in.)
17 Viola — mauve/blue, 2.5 cm (1 in.)

Trims

Dark elder buds, small leaves and stems.

DESIGN 7: FORMAL STAR DESIGN IN A ROUND FRAME

Colours

Blue, mauve, white, dark red and a touch of pink against an oyster background.

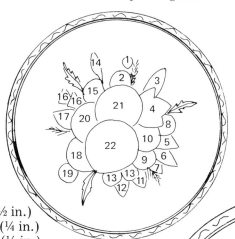

Flowers and foliage

1 Hellebore bud
2 Larkspur — blue,
  2 cm (¾ in.)
3 Grass head
4 Small ivy leaf
5 Anthemis leaf
6 Fern
7 Scilla — blue, 1.25 cm (½ in.)
8 Phlox — mauve, 0.5 cm (¼ in.)
9 Daisy — white, 1.25 cm (½ in.)
10 Hydrangea — pale blue, 1.25 cm (½ in.)
11 Rose leaf
12 Sage leaf
13 Scilla — blue, 1.25 cm (½ in.)
14 Lavender
15 Cineraria — dark red, 2 cm (¾ in.)
16 Scilla — blue, 1.25 cm (½ in.)
17 Grass head
18 Astrantia — green, 2 cm (¾ in.)
19 Phlox — mauve, 0.5 cm (¼ in.)
20 Hellebore — lilac, 5 cm (2 in.)
21 Anthemis — white, 4.5 cm (1¾ in.)
22 Hellebore — white, 5 cm (2 in.)

Figure 51   Filling in design 7

Finishing and framing

EQUIPMENT

For the free method

Pair of scissors for paper cutting
Glass cleaner and soft clean duster
Small paint brush, about 1.25 cm (½ in.)
Soft pencil and ruler
Gimlet or compass
Jeweller's small sharp-nosed pliers
Tacks (panel, veneer or gimp pins)
Small hammer
Wire/cord especially made for hanging pictures
Gummed paper strip, or sheet brown paper/wallpaper and
   a latex adhesive for finishing off
Two small picture rings with or without the loose rings

For the fixed method

As above, plus
Pair of sharp scissors for cutting material
Padding material (thin cotton wadding,
   old blanket, very thin foam)
Strong card or hardboard for backing

PREPARATION

The finishing off and framing up of a flower picture falls naturally into the area of pure craft. Patience and care are the first requisites, but it is worth making sure that you have the right tools for the job, for after that it will depend on neat fingers and a good eye. Try not to be in a hurry: you will need time to check and double check, and the one thing that you want to avoid is having to undo the back of a completed picture in order to put right a small error, and then having to frame it up a second time. Not only is this a time-wasting operation, but the flowers themselves are very delicate and can be spoiled. Additionally, if the free method of picture making is followed, they can actually move and the design may have to be repaired.

Always make sure, before you fix the flowers down, that the whole design rests exactly where you want it in the frame. It will be a continual source of visual discomfort if the design is either too high or too low in the frame, and disastrous if it is intended to lie centrally and is actually framed off-centre.

Never frame a design down if there is the slightest wrinkle showing in the background. It is essential that it is smoothed out and the excess fullness of material removed. Be very careful of designs with grasses and seed heads in them. The minute seeds have a habit of detaching themselves at the slightest provocation and of taking up a position in the most conspicuous place.

You will need a smooth-surfaced, firm table to work on, with a clean soft cover. An old cotton blanket will be ideal for this, for the frame will be upside down a lot of the time while you are working on the back and can very easily be spoiled by scratching. Gold frames, in particular, are very vulnerable, and the shining surface can be ruined by a few light scratches.

The jeweller's pliers mentioned in the equipment list are not absolutely essential — neat fingers will suffice — but they make things easier and are highly recommended. Make sure that the hammer you use is a really small one; some tack hammers are a bit too heavy for the job, particularly if the picture is small.

You may well have to shop around in order to get the right type and size of tacks or pins. Up to a point it will depend upon the size of the frame which size of pin will be suitable. There are several different types of small pins that you can use for holding the picture in its frame. Veneer or panel pins can be bought at hardware or DIY shops; these are usually silver in colour and have practically no head. Gimp pins and shoemaker's tacks are also small and suitable but have a much more pronounced head, and it is considerably easier if this is cut off with the pliers to begin with. These pins are made in small sizes ranging from 0.5 cm (¼ in.) upwards, but it is unlikely that you will need a size larger than 2 cm (¾ in.). Veneer and panel pins always have to be banged in with a hammer, but with the gimp or shoemaker varieties, which have a much sharper point, it is often possible to push them into the wood of the frame using the small pliers to hold them. This is of considerable advantage because the vibration caused by hammering will sometimes shift the loose flowers or dislodge miniscule pieces of leaf or stamen from the design.

When you are enquiring for the right type of pin, it is likely that you will be offered bayonet tacks. These have much larger heads to them and are generally much heavier. They are not suitable for this type of work even if the heads are removed.

Very small, sharp, metal triangles or diamonds are used a great deal in picture framing. They are about half the size of a little finger-nail and can be loaded into a spring gun which drives them with considerable force into the sides of the frame.

Before you begin work, make sure that your hands and the working surface are completely clean and dry. Clean the glass with a window cleaner and polish it well, and once it is spotless handle it only with the tips of the fingers on the edges or with the glass held between the palms of the hands: a finger-print inside the picture will show up when it is pressed against the background. Clean the frame itself well and ensure that the rebate is free from dust.

Eventually it will be necessary to cover the nails and the crack between the backing and the frame. Whether you cover the whole of the picture back with a single piece of strong paper (both brown paper and wallpaper are excellent), or whether you use a gummed paper strip around the edge is entirely a matter of personal choice.

FRAMING A DESIGN MADE BY THE FREE METHOD

1 The completed flower design is on its background in front of you. Take the paint brush and carefully brush the background surrounding the actual design free of all loose specks of dust and minute particles of foliage.

2 Clean the glass carefully and, holding it between the hands, place it gently on top of the picture, sliding it slowly if necessary, to match up the two shapes exactly.

3 Lay the frame on the top.

4 Hold the frame and backing tightly together and turn the whole thing over. The picture is now face downwards.

5 Take the hammer and four of the small pins, and hammer one into the inside edge of each of the four sides. You can hold the pin in your fingers, or alternatively you can use the little pliers. Always try to use as few strokes of the hammer as possible; the vibration caused by hammering can dislodge little pieces of debris that were lurking unknown in the flowers. Turn the picture over and inspect. Should this have happened, it is essential that you remove the pins, unframe the picture, brush the specks off and start again. If this difficulty occurs, always check to see that none of the flowers or leaves in the design itself has moved; the removing and replacing of glass can shift parts of the design considerably.

6 Hammer in more pins along each side of the frame. Common sense will guide you on this, but as a rough rule you will probably need about four pins along the side of a 20 cm (8 in.) frame — one pin about every 5 cm (2 in.) They must be banged in as close to the backing as possible and bent down onto the hardboard if necessary. They must not be left sticking out above it as otherwise they will not be exerting any leverage.

7 The picture must be held tightly against the glass so that the flowers are unable to move; it is most attractive when the

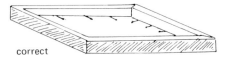
correct

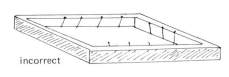
incorrect

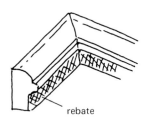
rebate

Figure 52 Inserting the pins into the frame

indentation of the flowers and leaves into the padding can be seen.

8 Make a final check for loose specks before papering the back. If the heads of the pins protrude slightly above the sides of the frame, run a strip of masking tape along the edges to cover them before you put on the paper.

9 Take a sheet of backing paper larger than the picture. Place the frame facing upwards on the paper and mark round with a pencil.

10 Cut just inside the pencil line with the scissors and stick carefully onto the back of the picture. A thin line of adhesive around the paper, smoothed out to the edges, with a second line across the centre will be sufficient. Smooth the paper down with a soft cloth. Alternatively, you can use gummed paper strip instead of the complete paper square. You will need a roll about 2.5 cm (1 in.) or 5 cm (2 in.) wide. Cut off four pieces the exact lengths of the sides of the frame. Moisten them with a wet cloth (do not lick) and stick them down neatly, each new piece overlapping the preceding one at right angles.

11 Make two small holes with a gimlet or compass point in the upright sides of the back of the frame, making sure that they are equidistant from the top. These are the holes for the screw eyes or picture rings.

12 Screw in two small eyes or picture rings, and thread a wire through them. Brass picture wire or nylon picture cord can be used for hanging. A double wire will be necessary for a heavy picture, while a few strands of twisted brass wire will be sufficient for a small one.

FRAMING A DESIGN MADE BY THE FIXED METHOD

1 Lay the picture in front of you on a clean working surface which is not too soft.

2 Clean the glass well and check that it fits the frame and is not too small. Place it over the design, then slide it about so that the design is at the right height, and adjust so that it is central.

3 Lay the frame over the top and readjust if necessary.

4 Remove the frame and check that the glass lies exactly on the cross-thread of the material at the base, and that the glass has no faults along the edges.

5 Hold the glass on firmly with one hand, and draw a pencil line around the edge of the picture.

6 Remove the glass, and using the sharp scissors cut exactly on the pencilled line.

7 Lay the glass on the padding, draw a line around it and cut out the shape. Repeat this procedure with several pages of magazine and lastly with thick cardboard if there is no

hardboard backing for the frame.

8 Remove any specks from the background of the picture.

9 Place the glass in the frame and lay the picture on it, making sure that the design lies the right way up in the frame.

10 Put the padding on next. If the design is a bulky one, take two of the shapes cut from the magazine and cut a similar-sized hole in the middle of each one (like an outsize corn plaster!). Place them over the padding and then put the remaining paper shapes into place.

11 Place the cardboard or hardboard on last, pinch it tightly together, and turn over. As in the other method of framing, the flowers should be pressed tightly against the glass so that you can see the effect of the padding.

12 Turn the picture back, lay it down on the soft surface and proceed with nailing up in exactly the same manner as described for the previous method. Paper the back of the frame similarly and add the picture rings and wire or cord.

FINISHING OFF

An excellent way to finish off the flower picture is to write on the back the details of where the flowers came from, the date the picture was made, and as a final point of interest you can add a full list of all the flowers used — with either their common or Latin names. Use a broad calligraphy nib and black writing ink; a really well-written and informative label will be much appreciated.

HANGING PICTURES

Hanging flower pictures is in some ways different from hanging other pictures. With landscapes, portraits and oil paintings you need to stand away from them to enjoy them fully. Seen from too close, the eyes can feel as if they were enduring somebody else's spectacles. Very close inspection, unless you are looking at brush strokes or the texture of the paint, is seldom rewarding. Flower pictures, however, take kindly to the most intimate appraisal. Indeed, viewed only from a distance most of the charm would be missed. So hang them at comfortable eye level and where you can get close to them. A pair, or even a group, of them can be attractive.

A flower picture is not great art and, of course, it would be presumptuous to pretend that it is. Do not hang it at the focal point of a room hoping that the picture will dominate it. Pressed flowers have no great message but are simply happy reminders of gardens and the countryside; things of beauty and of colour which will give lasting pleasure.

Further ideas for design

AESTHETIC AWARENESS

When you have made your first flower picture and hung it diffidently on the wall, people will look at it, admire it, and probably inspect it minutely. They will want to know how you made it and exactly how you pressed the flowers, where you found them and what their names are. These questions usually spark off a happy meeting of similar interests, and you will be able to explain your new skill with enthusiasm. People who have an inclination towards flowers and their beauty and who notice intricate detail and the blending of colours, those who appreciate skilful work and who are fascinated by botany — all these people will examine and enjoy your pictures. You will have created your pictures with an intention to produce perfection in the craftsmanship, and artistic awareness in the design.

Undoubtedly, pictures made at home differ greatly from the majority of pressed flower pictures on sale in the shops. Many of these are the products of commercial undertakings and should not be compared with the ones that are the subject of this book. They fall mostly into one of two categories: in the first, the pictures are completely mass-produced, usually comprising a pressed plastic frame, very shiny with artificial gold, a white card background and the minimum number of red, blue, white or yellow flowers; in the second variety, which owes much to the velvet and shine of the frames, the flowers hold their own only because they have surrendered their natural colour to artificial dyes.

We hope this book will provide many people with a first introduction to an absorbing and delightful occupation, and for those who aspire to the perfecting of it, this chapter will extend the subject and scope of ideas and encourage the reader to look for the artistic motive behind the design.

You find an old silver frame and polish it up until it shines brightly, and this will inspire you to hunt through your flower collection. Silver leaves and delicate white flowers? Perhaps a dark green background, but a green with a low sheen. You will have the silks around you and small suggestions of flower combinations on a piece of white card. You can place them this way and that, adding new colours, experimenting with fresh shapes on the silk, until you gradually achieve a balance of design within the shining frame that satisfies your eye.

It might be a group of leaves picked in the autumn which creates the idea for a design — the reds, browns and yellows tremendously evocative of that time of year. You search through your collection of frames and find a dark mahogany one. Rubbed up with furniture polish until the old patina shines again, it will hold them well. Brown satin is a possibility — a coffee brown? Perhaps it is a little too heavy, and a cream would be more of a contrast to the strong colours. Try some pale yellow rosebuds and some dark fine tendrils as an outline. Will a red wallflower be too strong? Cream grasses? Experiment all the time, avoid the makeshift solution, resist the temptation to reproduce the same style or size of design over and over again. There is a real danger here if you are making a large number of pictures for sale through a shop. You will then be one step away from the individual criticism or enthusiasm of a purchaser, and it is tempting simply to follow the type of design that you know will sell or be easiest and quickest to make. Put away your flowers and silks if you get stale and give yourself a rest for a month or two. After a winter's hibernation, a pretty frame and some flowers and ferns will spark off your imagination again in the spring, and you will find that ideas for designs will come easily. The following examples show how different effects can be produced by varying the approach to the basic design, capturing a different mood with each picture, and suiting the design to the frame.

Figure 53 Oval design in an antique frame

PICTURE 1: OVAL DESIGN IN AN 'ANTIQUE LOOK' FRAME

Flowers and foliage

Deutzia	Heuchera (red)
Scilla (blue)	Martagon lily
Alchemilla	Astrantia
Catmint	Candytuft
Purple verbena	Lavender
Anthemis cupaniana (white)	Hellebore (cream)
Viola (purple)	Auricula (yellow)
Forget-me-not (blue)	Hydrangea (blue)
Ipheion	Grasses (brown)
Tulip (miniature)	Elder buds
Primula (brown)	Willow leaves
Anthemis tinctoria (yellow)	Senecio
Hellebore (mauve)	Red maple

The frame

The frame shown in figure 53 is 35 x 25 cm (14 x 10 in.), and the moulding is 3.75 cm (1½ in.) in depth. It is a good quality, gold, wood frame, made in Italy and well finished. The gold has been given a final rubbing with a toothed implement so that in the very fine uneven lines around the oval the gold is slightly worn down and the dull brown-pink of the primer covering the gesso just shows through. A very fine spattering of black has been put over the gold, and this too has helped to break the intensity of the shine. This treatment gives the whole frame a successful 'old' gold-leaf finish.

The design

The flowers have been arranged in an oval, and all the points lying around the outline are equidistant from the frame edge. The background is ivory-cream silk dupion — the slub thread going across the picture. The colour scheme is unusual because there is virtually no green at all; all the natural foliage has been replaced by silver and silvery-green leaves. There are brown grasses and elder buds to help define the shape, and a spectacularly curly tendril on the right is balanced by the long stamens and pistil of a martagon lily on the left. Only three of the leaves are sharp and aggressive — a silver willow leaf at the top and two more at the base — the rest being deeply pinnate or gently ovate, mostly silver. The majority of the colours in this picture are soft shades which blend in with the grey foliage. There is bright blue in the scillas at the top and the base, while a small maple leaf, verbena and heuchera provide red with a good bite to it. The centre is built up to a cream hellebore and a mauve hellebore with two white daisy flowers of *Anthemis cupaniana* at the focal point.

Of technical interest, the strong lemon yellow of an *Anthemis tinctoria* is well overlapped by the colours mauve and white. If this had not been done, the vivid colour would have dominated the picture. A second point of interest is that the cream hellebore has been backed to overcome its transparency.

PICTURE 2: DESIGN IN AN ORIENTAL BLACK FRAME

Flowers and foliage

Mugwort	Hydrangea
Stinging nettle	Jasmine leaves
Passion flowers	

The frame

The picture shown in figure 54 has a narrow, black antique Chinese frame. It has rounded corners, measures 30 cm x 18.75 cm (12 in. x 7½ in.) and polishes beautifully to a high shine. Such frames are made of very hard wood indeed, such as ebony or lignum vitae, which makes framing up

Figure 54 Design in an oriental black frame

difficult. Pins can be used to hold the picture in place, but strong card should also be glued over the back to help hold the flowers against the glass and so give a padded effect.

The design

The colours used for this design were strong and simple — green, blue and cream against a pale cream furnishing fabric with the slub running across the picture. The leaves shown are from the ordinary climbing jasmine, clear and fine in outline and a dark olive green. This green is picked up by the black-green of the stinging nettle flowers and the paler grey green of the mugwort. There is a strong curve running down the design: the well-defined blue of the hydrangea florets surrounds the two passion flowers, and the paler of the two is backed, which helps it to stand out from the lower one and fixes the focal point.

PICTURE 3: LATERAL DESIGN IN A HEAVY FRAME

Flowers and foliage

Hydrangea (blue)
Agapanthus
Primula (brown)
Primrose (cream)
Wood anemone
  (European Anemone)
Astrantia
Martagon lily
Viola
Sorrel
Anaphalis
Mimosa (wattle)
Forget-me-not
Senecio
Wild strawberry

Hedge parsley
Lavender (mauve)
Potentilla (crimson)
Spiraea
Xeranthemum
Veratrum
Fern
Quaking grass
Maple
Ivy
Clematis montana
Potentilla anserina
  (silverweed, cinquefoil)
Grasses

The frame

The heavy, square Barbizon frame was bought at a sale room with its gilded surface in a very chipped state (figure 55). It was cut down to 32.5 cm x 25 cm (13 in. x 10 in.) external measurements and internal ones of 18.75 cm x 12.5 cm (7½ in. x 5 in.). The corners were well mitred, the surface cleaned, repaired and the whole repainted lightly with gold paint ('Renaissance Gold'). The dark crevices and indentations of the moulding have been allowed to stay as they were, and this prevents the gold surface from being too overpoweringly bright.

A very heavy antique gilt frame is used to make this picture. The cream satin background blends well with the gold of the frame. Amongst the flowers used are primroses, hydrangeas, potentilla, agapanthus and lavender. There is a martagon lily in the bottom right-hand corner. The small, dark, star shape at the top of the picture is a flower of *Veratrum nigrum* (false hellebore). The design has been arranged using the free method, and the padded backing presses the flowers against the glass.

Figure 55 Lateral design in a heavy frame

Figure 56 Bold design in a long frame

The design

The background is beige-cream satin, and the design has a good strength of colour. It is formal and solid in shape and so it holds its own with the frame. There are many different flowers, and the colours are completely mixed — green, mauve, blue and yellow, red and white — which gives the effect of a diminutive herbaceous border. The two lateral ferns are dark and give shape to the whole design.

PICTURE 4: BOLD DESIGN IN A LONG FRAME

Flowers and foliage

Anthemis (lemon yellow)	Fern
Anthemis (deep yellow)	Bracken
Xeranthemum	Willow
Feverfew	*Cineraria maritima*
Achillea (yellow)	Grasses
Silverweed (cinquefoil)	Anaphalis

The frame and design

This is a bold design put on a dark grey card. The frame has a cream-white modern moulding, and the whole measures 52.5 cm x 25 cm (21 in. x 10 in.). It can be hung either way, the design being a series of flowing curves. The colours are bright with two shades of yellow anthemis and shiny white xeranthemum, mixed with yellow achillea and feverfew. The leaves are an effective mixture of brown ferns, bracken and grasses with grey foliage.

PICTURE 5: LIVELY DESIGN IN AN OVAL FRAME

Flowers and foliage

Fuchsia	Hydrangea
Roses	London pride
Yarrow (milfoil)	Heuchera
Hellebore	Agapanthus
Astrantia	Chamomile
Martagon lily	Anthemis
Cow parsley (chervil)	Potentilla
Elderflower	Sorrel
Anaphalis	Astilbe
Japanese anemone	Xeranthemum
St Brigid's anemone	May
Heather	*Cineraria maritima*
Veratrum	Senecio
Polygonum	Willow
Wood anemone	Grasses
(European anemone)	Silverweed (cinquefoil)
Delphinium	Sage

Figure 57 Lively design in an oval Italian frame

The frame

The frame is 30 cm x 22.5 cm (12 in. x 9 in.), wooden and gold-leafed. It is Italian and very well made; the surface has a high sheen, but because it is only just over 1.25 cm (½ in.) wide it is not overpowering.

The design

The picture contains no less than thirty different flowers; despite this, the design has a feeling of great delicacy even though the background is of very dark green lining fabric (Milium). The overall colour scheme is of soft pale colours around the outside leading into the strong centre of red, mauve and blue. There is virtually no yellow in this design — only where it comes naturally in a few stamens.

There is a lively feeling about the whole picture, and this originates from the perimeter of the oval of flowers. It is broken by the movement of curled or twisted material, strongly indented leaves and skeletonized hydrangea petals — all these in pale colours which naturally silhouette against the dark green. The dipped and padded effect of the low sheen surface of the background fabric is pronounced in places, particularly around the finest of the stamens and tendrils. The 'action' of the edge of the design is picked up by the many graceful stamens of the mauve hellebore in the centre. The face of this flower is turned up a little, and this attracts the other flowers into the focal point.

PICTURE 6: LIGHT DESIGN IN A PANEL FRAME

Flowers and foliage

Geum	Clematis 'Comtesse de Bouchaud' (pink)
Ceanothus (blue)	Elderflower buds (black)
Mahonia japonica	

The frame

A long, panel picture, the frame is made of hard black wood. The back of strong card is firmly glued down and holds the flowers against the glass, and this gives enough of a padded effect. The background is a soft green-blue pure silk, with a good sheen and the slub going across the picture. The picture measures 60 cm x 11.25 cm (24 in. x 4½ in.)

The design

The colours are dark and are in strong contrast to the silk, the fine outlines of the elderflower buds, which are black when they are very small, appearing almost to be in silhouette. The colours become paler towards the centre with the pinkish-brown of clematis flowers. There are two firmly shaped heads of *Mahonia japonica* at the top and base of the

Figure 58 Light design in a panel frame

The black card background and narrow silver-painted frame form a dramatic surround to this white arrangement; the skeletonized hydrangea florets add lightness to the design.

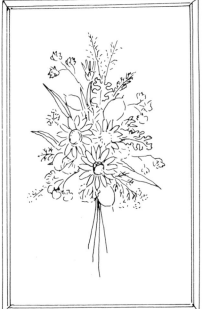

Figure 59   Bouquet design in a narrow frame

design. These are gold-yellow when growing but dry to a sombre blue-grey. Blue ceanothus gives a further blue to the panel centre, while geum heads provide some movement.

PICTURE 7: BOUQUET DESIGN IN A NARROW FRAME

Flowers and foliage

Honesty
Anaphalis
Skeletonized hydrangeas

Traveller's joy seed head   Willow leaves
Xeranthemum   Grasses

The frame and design

The modern silver frame measures 32.5 cm x 17.5 cm (11 in. x 7 in.). The background is black card, and the arrangement is white and silver with a great deal of shine to it. The effect is of dramatic contrast between the two surfaces, black and matt against the shining white and silver.

Various grasses and the points of willow leaves make an interesting outline, and the bright white flowers of xeranthemum a bold centre. Anaphalis, honesty and the skeletonized florets of hydrangeas complete the design. There is one fluffy seed head of traveller's joy to give weight to the base of the design.

DESIGNS WITH FLOWER VASES

One of the minor difficulties experienced in pressed flower arrangements is that one does not have the benefit of a vase to work from. There is no attractive bowl to hide the stems and to give the whole design a feeling of balance at the bottom. If you are doing a picture with this type of shaped arrangement, it is possible to manufacture a vase shape out of a suitable leaf or flower. Having said this, there is no doubt that a contrived effect of this nature will instantly give the design an appearance of artificiality which is never in nature itself and it will change the whole character of a picture. This is perhaps a question of botanical ethics versus personal choice, but it does raise a question in the mind of the purist.

Method

1 Select a suitable-sized leaf or flower (a small trumpet-shaped flower such as agapanthus or salpiglossis would be good) and cut the shape of your container neatly with a pair of scissors. Remember that a vase may need a small base to it. A leaf with vertical ribs such as a lily of the valley can also be used.

2 Place the vase in position on the material backing and then build the flower arrangement up above it. The proportions should be about two-thirds for the flowers to one-third for the vase in the overall height. If you have had experience in arranging fresh flowers, it will help you, for the same basic rules must apply. Make the outline first and then fill in towards the centre. All the flowers must appear to come from the vase.

3 Keep the bigger blooms low down and overlap some of them.

4 Break the top line of the vase by placing some of its 'contents' over it.

Figure 60 Balance the height of the arrangement with the height of the vase

Figure 61 Allow the flowers to overlap the vase to give a three-dimensional effect

87

An agapanthus flower is used to make this vase, a scilla making the base. A tendril from a passion flower plant is placed on the left to balance the pointed maple leaf on the right. A reversed raspberry leaf and mugwort flower are used to break the line of the container.

The vase is made from the leaf of a guelder rose, cut to shape. Dark leaves of fern and maple are used to tone with the container. The flowers include a primrose with a false centre of a cow parsley seed head, violas, forget-me-not, anaphalis and lavender.

Special subjects

HOLIDAY FLOWERS

Spring flowers from the high Pyrenees or from the low headlands of Malta in March, the heathers of western Scotland, or the shimmering profusion of Western Australia's flowers after the rain has come — it does not matter where you go or what you do, for when you are on holiday you will almost certainly see flowers that have such an alien charm that you will long to pick and preserve them. Painting and sketching can immortalize such beauty, but not everyone is gifted that way, and it is a slow pastime. Photography can capture it, but the equipment for close-up colour photography is expensive, and the results cannot be constantly displayed upon your wall for all to enjoy. But by pressing and arranging the flowers into delicate shapes, framing and labelling them, you will have a happy reminder of a good holiday. Next time you pack, take a small collecting box, blotting paper, and a little travelling press, and put them on the top of the suitcase or loose in the back of the car where you can reach them easily.

One of the most important things to remember is that wild flowers in all countries need protecting. Indiscriminate flower pickers can, at their worst, endanger rare species of flowers, or by sheer numbers spoil even the great carpets of colour such as are seen in bluebell woods in England. Take a small notebook, pencil and a flower recognition book with you. (It is not difficult to get paperback copies of reliable editions.) When you find a specimen that appears to be rare, restrain your hand, and leave it where it is. Always think before you pick for pressing, choose and cut carefully, and never pull the plant up. Remember the small leaves and buds for your picture and make a careful collection, being frugal and meticulous in what you put in the press. Try to identify them first and note the places where they were found.

In Britain, pressed flowers, provided they have no roots and soil attached, fall into the same category as cut flowers and so are exempt from restriction under the United Kingdom importing laws. Only if you are importing gladioli from Africa, Malta or Italy will the health authorities require you to get an import licence.

Pictures made from small collections of holiday flowers can be great fun for the family to collect. Malta or Madeira, Spain or California — all the flowers will mellow happily together. It is worth considering buying a long multiple mount and simple wood frame, using a neutral colour for the mount with small windows cut into it, so everybody may contribute a holiday bunch.

SPECIAL OCCASIONS

For a golden, silver or ruby wedding anniversary, a hundredth birthday or a coming of age a small picture is often an ideal present. With a little imagination, golden mimosa (wattle), buttercups and yellow doronicum flowers, mounted and framed by yellow and gold, can make a most appropriate golden wedding present. For a hundredth birthday, use a wide mount to encircle the flowers, and have the family's signatures radiating outwards on the mount; a personal present such as this can give an elderly person a great deal of pleasure.

New arrivals (using pink colours for a girl and blue for a boy), housewarmings, 'bon voyage' — there is endless scope for pictures, and they can also be made as gifts for the festivals throughout the year: Christmas, Easter, Mother's Day, St Valentine's Day, and so on. Christmas cards sent overseas are always much appreciated, for the flowers, even when they are pressed, really do remind people of the country from which they came.

WEDDING BOUQUETS

The idea that the younger generation of women are not as sentimental as their mothers and grandmothers is perhaps not always true, for the majority of young brides are only too pleased to have their bridal flowers pressed and arranged into a picture. There still seems to be an old-fashioned significance and sentimental attachment to these formal white arrangements of lily of the valley and white heather, and, no doubt, the age-old language of flowers still plays its part in the bouquets of some brides.

The wilting remains of a bride's bouquet, clutched by the warm hands of a small bridesmaid, and hurled happily into the air by the bride at the end of a long, hot summer wedding, will probably have to be kept until the next day before pressing. So put the flowers in a plastic bag and leave them to recover in as cool a place as possible; the refrigerator will do very well.

There is no point in unwinding the ribbons and starting to undo the handle end. Pick out the best blooms and begin by unwinding the fine wire the florist will have used to hold the flower heads upright. The wire will be wound round the stem and may well be threaded through the calyx itself,

92

and it will be a slow business disentangling the flowers. Each head will be wired onto a thicker strand of florist's wire, and this will lead down into the handle. Having got the blooms, leaves and buds off, lay them all on the blotting paper and consider them carefully. You will have only a very limited amount of material and you must make the best use of it.

White roses, gladioli, azaleas and freesias are all used and can be quite big flowers. If this is so, take a razor blade and cut them lengthways; the two halves will be much easier to press than the large heads, and you will have doubled the quantity. Put them in the press and name the sheet of blotting paper. Do not bother with gardenias or orchids unless you wish to tax your creative genius with some brown and reptilian-like blobs.

When you come to arrange the flowers, it may be worth asking the bride's mother if she has a small family frame that she would like used, and also if there is a suitable small piece of wedding dress material to use as a background. The colours of the flowers will have faded to the deep cream of old satin and lace, and they will be beautiful arranged on white with the darker shapes of the leaves. It will give the bride great pleasure — 'Modern Miss' though she is!

FLOWER FESTIVALS

Church Flower Festivals are becoming increasingly popular and anyone who presses flowers and takes an interest in them will welcome an opportunity to share in decorating a church. At first sight it might seem unlikely that such fragile echoes of three dimensional flowers would have any place beside large floral displays, and even pressed flower pictures would be out of keeping on the walls of a church, but there is one modest area where they come into their own and can add their own special beauty to a Festival of Flowers. Almost certainly your church will have a fine old Bible on the lectern and often a Book of Remembrance in a side chapel, and both can have decorative markers made from silk and pressed flowers. It is, of course, essential to obtain the permission of the priest or minister of the church first.

A Bible marker must of course be made to suit the size of the Bible, so it is not possible to dictate here exactly how long or wide that marker should be. First measure the Bible from the top to the bottom of the cover, double this measurement, and cut the material to this length. One half of the folded marker will lie inside the Bible, while the rest will lie over the top of the pages and be allowed to hang freely in front of the lectern, and it is only on this part of the marker that the flowers should be placed.

The size of the lectern must guide you as to whether you have a single marker or whether a pair will be more effective, and the actual width of the marker itself must also be depen-

(Opposite)
Flowers and leaves from a wedding bouquet arranged on a white silk background and ready for framing in an oval frame. The flowers include Christmas roses, lily of the valley, ivy leaves and rosemary, with small sprigs of scented-leafed pelargoniums.

dent upon the proportions of the Bible and the lectern. It is particularly important to realise that the design of flowers upon the material should be clearly defined both by colour contrast and outline if it is to have any visual impact for people sitting at a distance.

It is obvious that the fixed method must be followed when a Bible marker is being made and the instructions given on page 57 should be referred to. Any material can be used for making markers, but it should be remembered that they will be seen as part of the church hangings, and a pair of bright blue hessian markers for example, however attractive, will be sadly at odds with a fine altar frontal of scarlet silk damask. It is advisable, before buying your material, to find out which altar frontal and other hangings will be in use at the time of the Festival of Flowers.

A marker for a Book of Remembrance will be altogether a smaller affair, and since it will only be viewed from close to, the design can be as small, soft and intricate as you choose. The colours too need only be blended with the flowers in that area of the church. It is suggested that a very fine silk or cotton lawn should be used, because the pages of these books are invariably made of vellum or similar fine quality paper. Once again the dimensions of the marker must depend on the size of the book.

It will be seen from the illustration on the back cover of this book, that a 'pulled' self-fringe can be very effective, and in the following instructions for making a marker this type of fringe is envisaged.

Materials

The length of material for a Bible marker should be about double the measurement from top to bottom of the book. Allow for a turning at one end and for a fringe at the other.

The length for a marker in a Book of Remembrance needs only to be as long as the page it is to mark. Allow for the turning and the fringe.

The width of material should be two and a half times as wide as the finished marker is to be, plus a little extra for turning. It is essential that the material should be cut and folded exactly along the line of the threads, otherwise it may not hang straight.

A strip of iron-on interlining (such as Vilene), to stiffen the marker, can be cut the same length — minus the depth of the fringe, and fractionally less wide than the folded width of the marker.

Fringe

The fringe must be 'pulled' before the marker is made. Using the blunt end of a needle and starting at one edge of the material, pull and ease out the cross threads one by one until the required depth of fringe is made. Trim with small, sharp scissors.

Method

1 Place the strip of material face downwards on a clean surface.

2 Place the lining exactly along one long edge and above the fringe.

3 Run a line of tacking stitches down the centre of the lining.

4 Machine stitch the lining to the material across the non-fringe end of the marker, close to the edge.

5 Fold down the turning on the opposite long edge of the marker, tack, and iron flat.

6 Fold the marker inwards so that the stiffener is inside and the ironed edge runs smoothly down the centre back of the marker. Iron carefully.

7 Slip-stitch down, being careful not to catch right through the marker. (It is perfectly possible to stick the edge down with a thin application of adhesive (such as Copydex), instead of sewing it.)

8 Turn in the non-fringe end of the marker, tack and iron, then slip-stitch the edges together. Remove the tacking threads, and iron the whole marker carefully under a cloth. The marker is now ready for the flowers to be attached by the fixed method (see page 57).

SPECIAL SUBJECTS

To specialize in any subject is frequently more enjoyable for the person involved than for those called upon to admire. It is often so with flower pictures, and if you decide that your skill and imagination need stretching more fully, do not be disappointed if the finished results are not properly appreciated by others. Pictures of kitchen garden flowers are unusual and perhaps a little dull, but the fact is that it is quite a feat to create a picture at all out of the small flowers of potatoes, beans and radishes that does not resemble a compost heap! Rockery plants, herbs, grasses, or flowers month by month — this sort of thing is great fun to do if you enjoy a challenge to your ingenuity and demands made upon your time.

Suggestions for special subject pictures

Seasons of the year	Seaside flowers
Months of the year	Woodland flowers
Kitchen garden flowers	Flowers of trees or shrubs
Moorland flowers	Grasses

BOTANICAL PICTURES

Botanical pictures have been done for many years, and generations of children have learned the difference between a buttercup and a celandine because they picked them and were encouraged to press, mount and name them. The Victorians delighted in making up books of pressed flowers and they can still be found with the specimens faded but delightfully recognizable. The flowers were often arranged in fan shapes, and the stems at the bottom covered in pressed moss. Every page was accurately named using both Latin and English names. Such a book would be bound with leather and kept as a family heirloom.

It is well-worth starting a collection of a particular species and slowly adding to it over the years. Grasses would be excellent because they press splendidly and, mounted on a warm red background in a long frame, they will look very fine. Invest in a good-quality wood frame with a detachable back. The loose hardboard back will be held in place by swivel springs, and this means that you can keep on adding to your collection with the minimum of trouble. Make sure that you identify each variety accurately.

A small botanical picture is one of the simplest to make. You are limited by the specialist nature of the subject to a single type of plant, and the natural growth of it will guide you in making the design. Choose a frame accordingly and select flowers and leaves which will show the following botanical points: a flower in bud, a flower fully opened full-face and in profile; a young leaf in profile and one full-face, a mature leaf shown also in profile and in full.

Sometimes it is interesting to show a flower reversed showing the sepals and a reversed leaf to show any difference in colour. Show a seed head if possible. Some varieties of plants flower continuously over a period of time so that seeds and buds will be present on the plant together, and this too can be shown in the picture. With a minimum of three flowers and five leaves you will be able to design and make a botanical picture such as that shown in figure 62.

Figure 62 A small botanical picture of *Viola canina* (Heath dog violet), using an off-white background

Reconstituting, mounting and skeletonizing flowers

RECONSTITUTING FLOWERS

Even the best regulated press will sometimes yield up slightly spoiled flowers, and a bent petal will usually, although not always, show a line of fold if straightened out with the help of a warm iron. It is possible to remove the damaged petal and replace it with a perfect one from another imperfectly pressed flower.

Reconstituting a spoiled flower of *Helleborus niger*

1 Take two similar-sized flowers that have pressed badly.

2 Using the tweezers, carefully detach three good petals from flower A.

3 Detach two good petals from flower B and lay all to one side.

4 Choose the best pressed centre, and remove the rest of the petals from it.

5 Cut a square — a little larger than the flower — of thin white paper.

6 Put a circular dab of adhesive on the centre of the paper and spread thinly to about 1.25 cm (½ in.) in diameter.

7 Using tweezers, place the five petals on the glue, leaving a small space in the middle. (Use a complete flower here as a guide.)

8 Lastly place the free centre in the middle and press gently. Wait until really dry.

9 Using a small pair of scissors, cut the paper away carefully at the back, close to the base of the petals. The flower is now ready for use.

MOUNTING TRANSPARENT FLOWERS

Flowers with very thin petals can become semi-transparent when they are dried, and this means that a dark-coloured background will affect them in such a way that pieces of stem or leaf will show through. It is possible sometimes to overcome this difficulty by placing one flower directly on top of another of the same sort, but this is wasteful of flowers. The following method of mounting a thin-petalled flower will make it opaque.

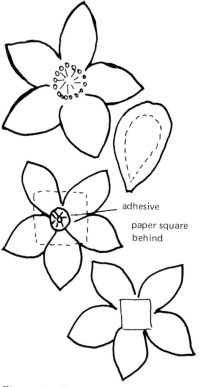

adhesive

paper square behind

Figure 63 To reconstitute a flower, detach the petals from the centre, trim each petal as necessary, then stick the petals one by one to a paper square, and stick the flower centre on last; then trim the backing paper neatly

Figure 64 To repair a flower with missing petals, stick spare petals from another flower onto a backing paper, stick the damaged flower on top, then trim the paper neatly

Figure 65 Trimming a helle-bore too large for the picture

Figure 66 Trimming an irregularly-shaped passion flower

Mounting a potentilla

1 Take one of the yellow flowers and remove the calyx (using tweezers).

2 Cut a circle of thin white paper a little bigger than the flower.

3 Put a small dab of adhesive in the centre and place the flower on it. Wait until it is completely dry.

4 With a small pair of pointed scissors cut the paper around the edge of the petals, just back from the edge.

5 Make sure that no paper sticks out beyond the petal line.

6 The flower is ready for use and will now be opaque.

ADAPTING

Flowers and foliage can be trimmed down in size to fit into an arrangement using a very sharp pair of scissors or a craft knife. This is particularly useful when flowers are irregular in shape or too large. Always be careful to follow the natural line of the petal or leaf (figure 65). It is also possible to combine part of one flower with part of another, such as adding a false centre of cow parsley seed head to a primrose or hydrangea. This practice may not be acceptable to the botanical purists, and is a matter of personal choice.

FADING

All flowers fade, and the bright sun is the greatest of the culprits. The vegetable dyes that are used in watercolour paints are affected as are those in plants, and both must be kept away from the strong sunlight. Like ageing beauties, let them both sit with their backs to the light!

SKELETONIZING

The fine tracery of the skeletons (i.e. the network of veins) of some leaves and flowers (such as hydrangea petals) are both effective and delicate when used in flower pictures. In skeletonizing, the intention is to soften and then remove all traces of the interlying tissue by the action of rapid decomposition in water, finally exposing the bleached tracery of the skeleton.

Skeletonizing hydrangeas

The so-called petals of hydrangeas are actually sepals and, therefore, constructed like a leaf with pithy veins. Use dry hydrangea florets — ones that have been in the house all the winter are ideal.

1 Put about ½ litre (20 fl. oz.) of water and three table-spoons of a detergent into a large saucepan. Drop the florets

in and let them simmer over a low heat for about an hour.

2 Strain them off with a wire sieve and rinse under the cold tap. (The tissue will now be soft.)

3 Tip the florets and loose petals into a bowl of cold water.

4 Extract them one by one on the tip of a finger and, using a soft toothbrush or a painter's hog's bristle brush, gently brush away the soft tissue. As the tissue comes away, the skeleton will appear underneath.

5 Transfer the leaves to clean blotting paper to dry. Patience is essential; the procedure is a little tedious, but well worthwhile.

PACKING AND POSTING

Broken glass in the post can ruin a picture. A safe way to pack it is to buy two small polystyrene (styrofoam) tiles and to place the picture between them. Fasten them together firmly and wrap the whole in corrugated paper. Label the package 'Glass with care'.

Figure 67   Trimming leaves to fit an arrangement

Appendices

Garden flowers for pressing

The following list of plants will make an excellent starting point when growing suitable material for pressing in your own garden, and the range will give a wide variety of colours, shapes, sizes and textures in both the flowers and leaves.

Spring flowering

Bulbs
snowdrop, small tulip, scilla, chionodoxa, narcissus

Perennials
lily of the valley, hellebore, primula, polyanthus, erica

Annuals and biennials
wallflower, forget-me-not

Summer flowering

Perennials
achillea, anaphalis, *Anthemis cupaniana*, *Alchemilla mollis*, feverfew, golden rod, astrantia, heuchera, miniature rose (single and double), viola

Annuals
lobelia, tagetes, *Phlox drummondii*, verbena, xeranthemum larkspur

Foliage plants, shrubs and climbers
Cineraria maritima, *Artemisia maritima nutans*, silverlace, fuchsia, *Clematis montana*, passion flower, Russian vine, ivy, deutzia, potentilla, hydrangea, guelder rose, *Kerria japonica*, 'Mermaid' rose, American Pillar rose, euonymus, Japanese maple (miniature)

Glossary of botanical terms

Anther The end of the stamen holding the pollen.
Biennial A plant that takes two years to complete its life cycle.
Bract A small unformed leaf near the flower head or at the base of the flower stalk.
Calyx The outermost whorl of the perianth. The leaf-like covering which encloses a bud and which lies at the back of the flower.
Corymb A flat topped cluster of flowers, the stalks of which arise one above the other from the stem.
Family A group of related plants.
Floret A small flower which is part of a cluster.
Frond The small leaf-like part of a fern.
Genus The smallest natural group containing related but distinct species.
Glaucous Covered with greenish-blue bloom.
Hirsute Hairy (usually soft).
Perennial A flower that lives for more than two years and usually flowers annually.
Perianth A complete floral envelope of petals and sepals.
Sepal A leaf of the calyx.
Species The basic unit of classification of plants.
Spur A slender projection at the back of the flower (sometimes hook-shaped).
Stamen One of the small delicate spikes lying in the centre of the flower (usually in a ring), carrying pollen at the top in the anther. Male reproductive organ.
Succulent Juicy.
Variety A distinct form of a plant.
Whorl A ring of petals, sepals or leaves around a stem, all at the same level.

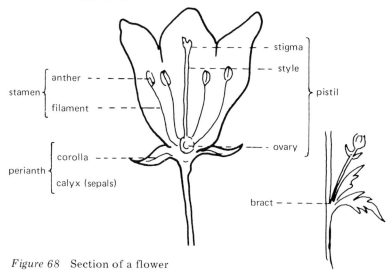

Figure 68 Section of a flower

Botanical classification

International botanical classification is by family, genus, species and variety. The variety (if any) is shown in quotation marks.

Family	Genus	Species
Snowdrop		
Amaryllidaceae	*Galanthus*	*nivalis*
Herb Robert		
Geraniaceae	*Geranium*	*robertianum*

Glossary of garden flowers

Symbols

A Annual	P Perennial
B Biennial	RP Rock plant
Bb Bulb	Sh Shrub
C Corm	T Tree
Cl Climber	Tb Tuber
H Hardy	W Wild
HH Half-hardy	

Acacia (Mimosa) T
A decurrens Bright yellow, small ball-like clusters. Buy from the florist in early spring.

Acer (Maple) T
The small-leafed Japanese varieties are the most suitable with their deeply indented red leaves.

Achillea (Yarrow) P
A. filipendulina The flowers, which are flat-headed, should be broken into small pieces and pressed separately. A good variety is 'Gold Plate' which has deep yellow flowers. *A. ptarmica* 'The Pearl' has small white flowers on large corymbs. Press singly and in groups. *A. millefolium* 'Cerise Queen' and *A. taygetea* 'Moonshine' produce cherryred and pale yellow flowers respectively.

Agapanthus (African lily) P
Flowers are deep violet-blue to pale blue, also white. Bell-shaped, borne in umbels on long stems. Press flowers individually, fully out and in bud. The 'Headbourne Hybrids' are fairly hardy and can be left out during the winter with a little straw as protection.

Ageratum HHA
A. houstonianum (Floss flower) Shades of mauve. Press individual flowers.

Alchemilla (Lady's mantle) P
A. mollis Flowers pale green. Press in small sprays. With the alpine species use only the leaves which are divided into separate leaflets. The reverse side has a silky, satin-like appearance.

Allium Bb
Flowers are star-shaped, borne on ball-like heads. Good species for pressing are the yellow *A. moly* and the pink *A. ostrowskianum*. Pick flowers off and press separately. Each floret is only about 1.25 cm (½ in.) across and when pressed is slightly transparent.

Alyssum (Sweet alyssum) HA
A. maritimum Heads of tiny flowers, pink, white or lilac. Press whole.

Amaranthus HA
A. caudatus (Love-lies-bleeding). Crimson and green. Press small trusses. Tends to lose colour when pressed.

Amelanchier (Snowy mespilus) T
A. canadensis Both blossoms and leaves are useful. Press the flowers in clusters and the bright red leaves in the autumn.

Ammobium HHA
A. alatum An everlasting flower. Pick the small daisy-shaped flowers when newly out. Needs heavy pressing as the flowers are quite thick and hard.

Anaphalis (Pearl everlasting) P
A. margaritacea and *A. triplinervis* Small clusters of white, button-like heads. Press some when in tight bud and others when fully out. Press some individually and some in clusters. (These make decorative centres for other flowers.)

Anemone Tb
A. blanda 2.5-5 cm (1-2 in.) across, colours white, pink, mauve, pale blue with yellow centres. Presses well, but be sure that the stamens are yellow. (This shows that the flower is fresh.) *A. coronaria* St Brigid can be grown in the garden. Presses well despite large, thick centres. Colours are strong and have to be used with care. (Flowers can be rather large; this can be remedied by trimming the petals.) *A. fulgens* has scarlet, ray petals with dark centre. Presses well and retains its vermillion colour. *A. hybrida* (Japanese anemone) P Pink or white, double or single. Press flowers, buds and leaves. (The centres are useful for using with other flowers.)

Anthemis P
A. cupaniana Large mats of silvery-grey, finely divided foliage. Flowers white, daisy-like, 2.5-5 cm (1½-2 in.) across. Press leaves and flowers. (Both are extremely useful and the flowers remain white.) Very easy to grow. *A. tinctoria* Pale lemon-yellow flowers.

Artemisia P (Wormwood)
A. absinthium (Lambrook silver), *A. abrotanum* and *A. maritima nutans* are all excellent for their feathery foliage. The leaves of *A. schmidtiana* are very delicate and useful.

Astilbe (False goat's beard) P
A. arendsii Shades of crimson, pink and white. White will turn cream when pressed. Press in small sprays.

Astrantia (Masterwort) P
A. maxima Pink or green with star-shaped flowers. Useful for its unusual shape.

Auricula *see* Primula

Bleeding Heart *see* Dicentra

Briza (Quaking grass) HA
B. maxima and *B. minor* are both very useful. Easily grown from seed.

Calendula (Marigold) HA
C. officinalis Will press satisfactorily, but the petals may shrink. Use one flower on top of other.

Candytuft *see* Iberis

Caryopteris Sh
C. clandonensis Flowers are mauve in small clusters. Press whole. The leaves are pointed with grey undersides.

Catmint *see* Nepeta

Ceanothus Sh
Fluffy flowers in small spikes, pale to deep blue.

Chionodoxa (Glory of the snow) Bb
C. luciliae Blue star-shaped flowers with white centres.

Christmas rose *see* Helleborus

Chrysanthemum HA
C. carinatum The flowers are bright with rings of yellow, purple and red. *C. segetum* 'Eastern Star' and *C. coronarium* 'Golden Glory' are both yellow. *C. parthenium* (Feverfew), white and much smaller, with a yellow centre, is very useful. *C. haradjanii* Rp Use leaves only — small, grey, fern-like.

Cineraria *see* **Senecio**

Clary *see* Salvia

Clematis Cl
C. montana Press the flowers and the leaves when they are small. The leaves turn nearly black when dry and have a satin-like sheen. Very useful. Any small-flowered clematis will press well.

Clerodendron T
C. trichotomum Press the white star-like flowers in clusters. When the flowers are over, remove the turquoise-blue berry and press the star-shaped crimson calyx.

Convallaria (Lily of the valley) P
C. majalis Excellent for pressing. Press the whole stem of flowers which will turn cream when dry. Press leaves too.

Cowslip *see* Primula

Crocosmia C
C.x crocosmiiflora (Garden montbretia). Small orange flowers growing in arching sprays. Press separate flowers and sprays of buds.

Crown Imperial *see* Fritillaria

Cynoglossum (Hound's tongue) P
C. nervosum Similar to the forget-me-not. Press small sprays of this deep blue flower.

Delphinium HA
D. ajacis (larkspur) Tall spikes of blue, mauve, pink and white. Press individual flowers, sprays or buds from the tip of the plant and also the profiles of flowers. Keeps colour well. After pressing some petals may have to be removed to expose the centre. Flowers tend to be a little shapeless. Belladonna hybrids P Blue, pink and white. Presses well but also a little shapeless. Use the smaller flowers.

Deutzia Sh

Many varieties are suitable. Pink and white clusters of small star-shaped flowers. Press whole sprays with buds and also individual flowers.

Dicentra P

D. spectabilis (Bleeding heart, Dutchman's breeches)   Use for its unusual pink and white heart-shaped flowers. Press in sprays.

Doronicum (Leopard's bane) P

D. cordatum   Daisy-shaped yellow flowers which press well. It may be necessary to use one superimposed on the other as the petals are apt to look a bit thin.

Edelweiss *see* Leontopodium

Elaeagnus Sh

E. pungens   'Maculata'. Shiny, dark green leaves which are splashed with golden yellow at the edges. Choose differing sizes for pressing. The underside of the leaf is useful for its rusty appearance.

Elder *see* Sambucus

Epimedium (Barrenwort, Bishop's hat) P

E. pinnatum   Sprays of small yellow or pink flowers. The leaves, which are heart-shaped, turn bronze in autumn. Press both flowers and leaves.

Erica (Heather) P

Pinks, whites and mauves. Presses well, but the small leaves are inclined to drop off. Before using in a picture shake off the loose leaves.

Euonymus Sh

E. fortunei   'Variegata' Evergreen. Small oval leaves, green and white. Some turn pink in the winter.

Euphorbia (Spurge) P

E. fulgens   A greenhouse variety. It can be bought early in the year from florists and has small single vermilion flowers about 1.25 cm (½ in.) in size, along the stem. These can be picked off and pressed individually. The bright colour will keep remarkably well. *E. polychroma (E. epithymoides)* Pick the bright lime-yellow bracts in spring. Press whole; they can be separated when dry for use. *E. pulcherrima* (poinsettia) Scarlet, white and pink. Use the smaller 'petals' from the bracts. The colour is retained very well.

Exochorda Sh

E. giraldii   Masses of small white flowers along the branches, particularly useful for the sprays of buds.

Fern P

Many varieties. All press well (with the exception of *Phyllitis scolopendrium* (hart's-tongue))

Feverfew *see* Chrysanthemum

Flowering Currant *see* Ribes

Forget-me-not *see* Myosotis

Freesia C

All shades of yellow, pink and mauve. Press singly and in sprays.

Fritillaria Bb

F. imperialis   Bisect each flower and press.

Fuchsia Sh
There are many varieties. The common *F. magellanica* presses extremely
well and retains its colour. Some of the bigger and fatter ones should
be bisected. It is essential that the attractive, long, hanging stamens
and pistil are retained as these comprise half the beauty of a fuchsia
in a picture.

Funkia *see* Hosta

Galanthus (Snowdrop) Bb
G. nivalis   Single and double flowers. Press full face and in profile.

Gentiana (Gentian) P
Bright blue. All varieties are good for pressing.

Geranium (Cranesbill) P
Not to be confused with the bedding geranium, *Pelargonium. G. sanguineum* which is a deep magenta colour, is excellent.

Golden Rod *see* Solidago

Grasses P
There are many species of grasses most of which press very well. *Briza*
(quaking grass) and *Lagurus ovatus* (hare's tail) are most attractive.

Guelder Rose *see* Viburnum

Gypsophila HA and P
G. elegans   Pinks and whites, some double. Pick and press small pieces.
G. paniculata Press in sprays.

Heather *see* Erica P

Hedera (Ivy) Cl
Many species, both green and variegated. Use leaves, flowers and
berries.

Helianthemum (Rock rose) Sh
Flowers can be white, yellow, orange or crimson. Presses well.

Helleborus (Christmas rose) P
There are several species of the hellebore. The white *H. niger* (Christmas
rose) flowers during the winter. The green ones *H. viridis, H. foetidus*
and *H. corsicus* flower in early spring, as does *H. orientalis* (Lenten
rose) in shades of both dark and light mauve and white. All press
very well. Old white hellebore flowers may turn green on the plant.
Pick at this stage as well and press.

Heuchera (Coral flower) P
H. sanguinea   Delicate sprays of pink or red flowers. Press whole
sprays and small pieces. Keeps colour well.

Honesty *see* Linaria

Honeysuckle *see* Lonicera

Hosta (Funkia) P
There are many species, but only flowers are suitable for pressing
(leaves tend to be too big). The colour will turn from cream to brown.

Hydrangea Sh
White, pinks and blues. All keep their colour very well. Pick when in
full colour and later when some have turned green.
H. petiolaris Cl , the climbing white species, is also good for pressing.
Pick when young flowers are white, also when green. When dry,
hydrangea flowers can be skeletonized.

Hypericum (St John's wort) Sh
H. olympicum   Use only small varieties for pressing. The central boss of golden stamens is most effective.

Iberis (Candytuft) HA
Flat heads in shades of purple, mauve, pink and white. Pick heads of differing sizes and press whole.

Ipheion Bb
I. uniflorum (Spring star flower)   The flower is star-shaped when fully out, with a dark line down the centre of each petal. Slightly transparent when pressed.

Iris P
I. reticulata Bb and *I. tuberosa* Tb (Snake's head iris)   These press well. (The larger species are not really suitable for pressing.)

Ivy *see* Hedera

Jasminum (Jasmine) Sh
J. nudiflorum (winter jasmine)   Yellow star-like flowers. Useful for pressing in the winter. It is advisable to place sprays of flowers in a vase for several hours to allow flowers to dry completely before pressing. *J. officinale* Cl (common jasmine) A climber. Useful for very small flowers. Press in profile and full face with the tube cut off. Leaves exceptionally good.

Lamb's Tongue *see* Stachys

Larkspur *see* Delphinium

Lavandula (Lavender) Sh
L. spica (old English lavender)   Very useful for making a pointed shape. Pick when tips are still in bud.

Leontopodium (Edelweiss) P
L. alpinum   Silvery-grey velvety flower which presses well. Useful for its grey colour.

Leucojum (Snowflake) Bb
L. vernum (spring snowflake)   Similar to the snowdrop but larger, with green tips at the end of petals.

Lilac *see* Syringa

Lilium (Lily) Bb
There are many species of lily, the smaller ones of which will press well. Bisect the flower and press both halves, taking care to retain the pistil and stamens. *L. martagon* and *L. pyrenaicum* (yellow Turk's cap lily) press extremely well, the former turning pale brown and the latter retaining its yellow colour. Do not press the large species.

Lily of the Valley *see* Convallaria

Limnanthes HA
L. douglasii (Poached egg flower)   Yellow, five-petalled flower edged with white.

Limonium (Sea lavender, statice) HHA
L. sinuatum   Known as 'everlasting' flowers, mixed colours. Flowers can be picked off and pressed individually, and the bright colour will be retained.

Linaria (Toadflax) HA
L. maroccana   Flowers resemble miniature snapdragons and have a similar colour range. Press in profile.

Lobelia HHA
L. erinus Various shades of blue. Useful for small arrangements.

London Pride *see* Saxifraga

Lonicera (Honeysuckle) Cl
L. americana Press in profile. Flowers turn pale brown. Useful shape.

Love-in-a-mist *see* Nigella

Love-lies-bleeding *see* Amaranthus

Lunaria (Honesty) HB
L. annua Use dried seed head. Slip off outer covering to reveal a silvery satin skin. Unnecessary to press as it is already flat.

Maple *see* Acer

Marigold *see* Calendula and Tagetes

Mimosa *see* Acacia

Montbretia *see* Crocosmia

Muscari (Grape hyacinth) Bb
M. armeniacum Bright blue, small bell-like flowers in tight clusters. Press whole stem and seed heads. Keeps colour well.

Myosotis (Forget-me-not) HB
M. alpestris All shades of blue, also white and pink. Press small sprays. The end buds curl very attractively.

Myrtus (Myrtle) Sh
M. communis Small, shiny pointed leaves. Small white flowers with numerous stamens.

Narcissus Bb
N. tazetta Press the narcissi with small trumpets such as 'Paper White' and 'Grand Soleil d'Or'. Before pressing clip round trumpet using small scissors, then press flat. Only the smallest varieties of daffodils should be pressed. Bisect through flower and calyx and press both halves in profile.

Nepeta (Catmint) P
N.x faassenii Feathery spikes of pale purple flowers. Tends to fade.

Nerine Bb
N. bowdenii Deep pink which turns deeper when pressed. Shape attractive.

Nicotiana (Tobacco plant) HHA
N. affinis The green and white varieties are best. Cut off the trumpets and press flat.

Nigella (Love-in-a-mist) HA
N. damascena Mostly blue. Fades when pressed. Shape attractive.

Ornithogalum (Star of Bethlehem) Bb
O. umbellatum White flowers with pointed petals which bloom in spring. *O. thyrsoides* (chincherinchee) is a native of South Africa and can be bought in winter from the florists. It has many flowers on long stems, and these should be pressed separately. They become rather transparent when dry and may have to be mounted. *O. nutans* is an attractive species with a green line running down the centre of each petal.

Pansy *see* Viola

Parthenocissus (Virginia creeper) C1
Used for its leaves which turn red in autumn. Choose small ones and terminal sprays.

Passiflora (Passion flower) C1
P. caerulea Presses very well and adds importance to an arrangement because of its unique shape. Pistil, stamens and sepals must be removed and pressed separately. Use tendrils and small leaves too.

Phlox HHA
P. drummondii In varying colours from white to deep crimson.

Polygonum (Russian vine) C1
P. baldschuanicum Press small spikes of flowers which curl into attractive shapes.

Potentilla (Cinquefoil) P
P. atrosanguinea Bright scarlet five-petalled flowers which turn maroon when pressed. The variety 'Gibson's Scarlet' is well-worth growing for pressing.
P. fruticosa, Sh, a cream-yellow shrub species, produces flowers which tend to fall apart when pressed.

Primula P
The polyanthus and the common Primulaceae — cowslips and primroses — are all most useful for their varied colours. Press in profile, full face (having first removed the sepals) and also in bud. The auriculas come in many bright colours — yellows, mauves, deep crimsons and pinks with yellow and white centres — and are a most suitable shape for pressing.

Pulsatilla P
P. vulgaris (Pasque flower) Pink-mauve and white. Has soft silky petals and deeply indented leaves.

Pyrethrum P
P. ptarmicaeflorum 'Silver Lace', very finely cut silvery grey leaves. Extremely useful.

Quaking grass *see* Briza

Raspberry *see* Rubus

Rhus (Sumach) Sh
R. cotinus Leaves are deep purple, and the fluffy flowers can be used too.

Ribes (Flowering currant) Sh
R. sanguineum Pink or red flowers in small sprays. Press whole sprays.

Rock Rose *see* Helianthemum

Rosa (Rose) Sh
Press small species single and double. The single 'Canary Bird' and 'American Pillar' and miniature varieties are excellent. Small, double roses should have some of the centre petals removed before pressing to reveal the stamens. Press buds and leaves.
The dog rose, *R. canina*, also presses well but goes cream.

Rubus Sh
R. idaeus (raspberry) Press young small leaves for the silver colour on the reverse side.

Rue *see* Ruta

Russian vine *see* Polygonum

Ruta (Rue) Sh
R. graveolens Useful for the colour of the blue-grey divided leaves.

Sage *see* Salvia

Salix (Willow) T
S. alba The pointed leaves of the willow are most useful, particularly those of *S. alba* which are grey with silvery white undersides.

St John's Wort *see* Hypericum

Salpiglossis HHA
S. sinuata Crimson, yellow, mauve, violet and sulphur coloured, trumpet-shaped, beautifully veined flowers. Very suitable for making 'vases'.

Salvia (Sage) Sh
S. officinalis (common sage) The grey leaves press well as do the small flowers freshly cut.
S. horminum HA has coloured bracts which are mauve or purple.
S. sclarea (clary) HB The tops when pressed will form rosettes.

Sambucus (Elder) T
Clusters of buds in early spring turn nearly black when pressed. Press clusters of flowers too.

Santolina (Cotton lavender) Sh
S. chamaecyparissus Use the grey feathery leaves.

Saxifraga P
The Kabschia saxifrages are grown on rockeries, small single flowers colours pink, white and yellow. *S. umbrosa* (London pride) has small delicate stems of flowers. Press whole heads.

Scabiosa (Scabious) HA
S. atropurpurea Press whole heads. Remove petals and press the pretty star-shaped calyx.

Scilla Bb
S. bifolia Star-shaped flower, generally royal blue which keeps its colour well.

Senecio Sh
S. greyi Evergreen shrub with grey leaves. Press leaves only. *S.* 'White Diamond' is grown as a foliage plant for its silvery-white leaves.
S. cineraria maritima HHP The pale grey, deeply cleft leaves are a must for their beautiful silvery colour.
S. cruentus (Cinerania multiflora) HHA is sold as a pot plant. It has brightly coloured daisy-shaped flowers which press fairly well. The petals tend to shrink. Use one flower on top of another.

Snowdrop *see* Galanthus

Solidago (Golden rod) P
Yellow panicles of small flowers. Press small sprays.

Spiraea Sh
S. japonica 'Anthony Waterer'. Small shrub with rosettes of small pink flowers which turn brown when pressed whole. Press the leaves which are sometimes pale pink and cream

Spurge *see* Euphorbia

Stachys P
S. lanata (Lamb's tongue). A plant grown for its silvery grey leaves which have a velvety texture. Press small leaves only.

Statice *see* Limonium

Stephanotis Cl
S. floribunda White, waxy flowers — used in bride's bouquets — which are obtainable from florists. Goes creamy when pressed.

Syringa (Lilac) T
S. vulgaris White, pale and deep mauve. There are also a number of varieties, and a yellow one called 'Primrose'. Press small trusses and single flowers. All tend to turn brown but are useful for their shape.

Tagetes (Marigold) HHA
T. tenuifolia (T. signata) Small flowers of orange or strong yellow. Press in profile and full face. Leaves, which are delicate and a fresh green colour, press well.

Thymus (Thyme) P
T. serpyllum Some have variegated leaves. Flowers and leaves are excellent for pressing.

Tiarella P
T. wherryi Heart-shaped leaves with dark veins. Cream feathery flowers on spikes. Press leaves and flowers.

Tobacco plant *see* Nicotiana

Tulipa (Tulip) Bb
Some of the small flowers which grow up beside the parent plant are excellent, bisected or whole. Most tulips are too large.

Veratrum P
V. nigrum Almost black star-shaped flowers growing up long spikes. One stem will yield several dozen small 1 cm (½ in.) flowers, which go completely black when dry.

Verbena HHA
V. hybrida Mixed colours and white, in clusters. Press whole heads and single flowers.

Viburnum Sh
V. opulus (guelder rose) Balls of white single flowers. Press small clusters. These can be separated for use later. *V. carlesii* Press individual flowers.

Viola P (Pansy)
Select flowers for pressing that have very definite colours such as mauve and yellow, and brown and yellow. Small flowers of a single colour also press well, although they may lose their shape. Use flowers with pleasant expressions only!

Virginia creeper *see* Parthenocissus

Wind flower *see* Anemone

Willow *see* Salix

Xeranthemum HHA
X. annuum Everlasting daisy-like flowers, pale lilac and white with a permanent satiny sheen. Most effective in arrangements.

Yarrow *see* **Achillea**

Glossary of wild flowers

Flowers

Agrimony
Agrimonia eupatoria Yellow. June-August. Yellow flowers on spikes. Good for pressing. Effective shape.

Anemone, Wood
Anemone nemorosa White. March-April. Colour deepens to cream when dried; small leaves a good shape.

Angelica *see* Umbelliferae

Asphodel, Bog
Narthecium ossifragum Yellow. July-September. Yellow flowers on small spikes. Excellent for pressing. Leaves also good.

Autumn Squill *see* Squill

Barren Strawberry *see* Strawberry

Birdsfoot Trefoil
Lotus corniculatus Yellow. June-August. Flowers and buds good for pressing. Press whole and look for colour variation.

Blackberry
Rubus fruticosus Spring-autumn. Flowers in spring; leaves particularly good when coloured in autumn.

Black Medick *see* Medick

Bluebell
Endymion non-scriptus Blue. May-June. Buds only for pressing. Colour fades.

Bracken
Pteridium aquilinum May-October. Fronds can be pressed at various stages during the year. Particularly useful for colours in autumn.

Broom
Sarothamnus scoparius Yellow. May-June. Broom tends to dry dark brown or even black. Press flowers singly and also the tips of the flowering stems.

Bryony, White
Bryonia dioica Green/white. May-August. Unusual for colour. Tendrils and small leaves are particularly useful.

Buttercup, Meadow
Ranunculus acris Yellow. April-September. Buds and flowers are excellent for pressing. (Old flowers will fade to white when dry.)

Campion, Red
Melandrium dioicum Red. May-October. Flowers are a little difficult to press, but the colour is good.

Celandine, Lesser
Ranunculus ficaria Yellow. March-May. Buds and young flowers press well. Old flowers dry nearly white.

Chamomile, Corn
Anthemis arvensis White/yellow centre. June-July. Flowers very effec-

tive when pressed well. Place flower heads on blotting paper well away from each other and press tightly. Petals tend to shrivel. Unusual leaf shape.

Chives
Allium schoenoprasum Purple/pink. June-July. Cut florets off flower heads and press singly. Very small and delicate but they press well.

Cinquefoil, Creeping
Potentilla reptans Yellow. June-September. Flowers can be difficult since the petals may drop. Small leaves are excellent.

Coltsfoot
Tussilago farfara Yellow. March. Press flowers and buds, full face and profile.

Columbine
Aquilegia vulgaris Pink, white or purple. May-June. Full face is difficult; flower profile gives unusual shape. Buds are useful.

Comfrey
Symphytum officinale Cream or purple. May-June. Flowers press well in profile only. The cream colour darkens when dry. Good shape.

Common Rue *see* Rue

Cornflower
Centaurea cyanus Blue. June-August. Florets can be pressed separately; the colour is unusually good. Buds and small leaves.

Cow Parsley *see* Umbelliferae

Cowslip
Primula veris Yellow. April-May. Presses well. Usually necessary to cut florets off and press separately.

Cranesbill (Herb Robert)
Geranium robertianum Red or pink. April-October. Flowers, buds, leaves and seed heads are all excellent for pressing.

Creeping Cinquefoil *see* Cinquefoil

Daisy
Bellis perennis White/pink. All year. Press flowers full face and profile.

Devilsbit Scabious *see* Scabious

Fennel *see* Umbelliferae

Flax, Perennial
Linum perenne Blue. May-August. Press whole flower sprays, allowing tips to curl over. Excellent.

Fleabane
Pulicaria dysenterica Yellow. August-September. Press flowers full face and profile. Needs very hard pressing.

Flowering Rush *see* Rush

Geum
Geum rivale Pink/brown. May-September. The heads of the flowers and buds hang down and are very attractive when pressed. Seed heads also good.

Groundsel
Senecio vulgaris Yellow. All year. Buds, flowers and seed heads all press well.

Heartsease
Viola tricolor Yellow/purple/white. April-September. Flowers press well. Cut the stem off close to the flower and press separately. Buds are attractive for shape.

Heather
Erica Pink and purple. July-September. All flowers press well, but the leaves tend to drop.
Calluna vulgaris Mauve/pink. July-September. Presses very well indeed, and these leaves do not drop.

Herb Robert *see* Cranesbill

Ivy
Hedera helix Evergreen. Press small leaves, useful for their shape. Seed heads can be pressed whole.

Ivy-leafed Toadflax *see* Toadflax

Lady's Bedstraw
Galium verum Yellow. July-August. Flowers and foliage dry dark green or black. Most useful for colour and delicate tracery.

Lady's Smock
Cardamine pratensis Pink/white. April-June. Press flowers separately. Clusters of buds useful.

Lesser Celandine *see* Celandine

Mallow
Malva sylvestris Purple/pink. June-September. Flowers only, useful colour.

Meadow Buttercup *see* Buttercup

Meadowsweet
Filipendula ulmaria Cream. June-August. Press clusters of fully opened flowers. Small buds excellent for colour and shape. Dries brown/black.

Medick, Black
Medicago lupulina Yellow. May-August. Small yellow flowers, unusual shape in flower and seed heads.

Melilot, Ribbed or Common
Melilotus officinalis Yellow. June-September. Useful flower spikes. Presses well.

Milkwort
Polygala vulgaris Blue. May-September. Excellent for colour, delicate shape.

Mugwort
Artemisia vulgaris Grey-green. July-September. Spikes of flowers are useful. Leaves are dark green with silver-grey on the reverse side.

Nettle, Stinging
Urtica dioica Green. All year. Press the top clusters of small leaves and flowers; they will dry dark green or black. The long tassels of flowers are very effective for shape and colour.

Perennial Flax *see* Flax

Poppy, Common Red, Corn
Papaver rhoeas Red. June-August. Petals tend to dry transparent and will need backing. Buds and seed heads are useful but need bisecting.

Primrose
Primula vulgaris Yellow. February-May. Press buds and flowers. Sometimes necessary to trim the back of the flower before pressing.

Ramsons
Allium ursinum White/green streaks. April-June. Press florets singly, full face and profile. A little transparent but effective.

Ragged Robin
Lychnis flos-cuculi Red. May-June. Difficult to press but good colour.

Red Campion *see* Campion

Rose-bay *see* Willow-herb

Rock Rose
Helianthemum chamaecistus Yellow. June-September. Flowers fragile and difficult, inclined to stick to blotting paper. Most useful when successful. Tips of flowering stems with buds are excellent.

Rock Stonecrop *see* Stonecrop

Roses, Wild
Rosa Pinks and white. Mostly June-July. Nearly all worth pressing. tend to dry dark cream or brown. Very effective when the centre dries an even darker shade. Buds and small leaves also excellent. (Bisect the buds before pressing unless they are very small.)

Rue, Common Meadow
Thalictrum flavum Green/yellow. June-July. Press sprays. Useful shapes. Tends to dry darker.

Rush, Flowering
Butomus umbellatus Pink. July-September. Cut florets and press separately. Excellent.

Scabious, Devilsbit
Succisa pratensis Blue/purple. June-October. Flowers need hard pressing. Small flowers and buds are best.

Sea Lavender
Limonium vulgare Mauve/white. July-September. Good for pressing. Detach and press small sprays.

Shepherd's Purse
Capsella bursa-pastoris White. All year. Press small seed heads only. Traditional 'purse' shape.

Silverweed
Potentilla anserina Yellow. July-August. Flowers not easy since the petals tend to fall off. Leaves delicate and excellent.

Sneezewort
Achillea ptarmica White. July-August. Press flowers singly or in small groups, also bud clusters and small leaves. All press well and are extremely useful.

Sorrel, Sheep's
Rumex acetosella Red/green. May-August. The dark red or green spikes are very effective and press well. (Larger varieties of sorrel such as the common sorrel, *Rumex acetosa*, tend to drop the florets and seeds when dry.)

Squill, Autumn
Scilla autumnalis Deep blue. July-September. Excellent for pressing.

Squill, Spring
Scilla verna Pale blue. April-May. Good for pressing.

Stonecrop, Rock
Sedum forsteranum Yellow. June-July. Surprisingly good flowers for pressing. Leaves too fleshy. Press flower heads whole.

Strawberry, Barren
Potentilla sterilis White. February-May. Leaves useful.

Strawberry, Wild
Fragaria vesca White. April-July. Flowers and leaves press well. Small garden fruits are very effective when dry. Bisect if necessary.

Tansy
Chrysanthemum vulgare (Tanacetum vulgare) Yellow. July-September. Solid little flowers which require heavy pressing. Do not crowd on blotting paper. Press singly.

Thrift
Armeria maritima Pink. May-September. Flowers press well.

Thyme, Wild
Thymus serpyllum Mauve/pink. June-September. Presses quite well. Colour of flowers a little unreliable, but the whole stems give an attractive shape.

Toadflax, Ivy-leafed
Cymbalaria muralis Mauve/white. April-November. Very small delicate plants. Press curled stem of flowers and leaves whole.

Traveller's Joy
Clematis vitalba Green/white. July-September. Flowers, buds and leaves are all excellent. Leaves dry dark green or nearly black.

Umbelliferae
Mainly white, but some yellow or pink-mauve. A large family. It is difficult to distinguish between some varieties. Flowers and small leaves press well, and the seed heads are usually excellent, drying a very dark shade of green or black.
Angelica *Angelica sylvestris* White or pink. July-September. Cut florets off and press separately.
Cow parsley or Queen Anne's lace *Anthriscus sylvestris* White. April-June. Presses very well indeed.
Fennel *Foeniculum vulgare* Yellow. July-September. Presses well, useful for its colour.

Valerian, common
Valeriana officinalis Pink/mauve. June-September. Difficult to press as the flowers are small and bunched together. They dry rather dark. Press small clusters.

Vetch, Bush
Vicia sepium Blue. April-October. Flowers press well.

Vetch, Tufted
Vicia cracca Blue. June-August. Flowers and buds press well. The fine tendrils are particularly useful.

Violets, Wild
Viola Blue, purple and white. April-June. A large family. The flowers

press well on the whole, particularly in profile. Buds and small leaves are also useful.

White Bryony *see* Bryony

Wild Strawberry *see* Strawberry

Willow-herb (Rose-bay)
Epilobium angustifolium Pink/purple. July-September. Single flowers full face and profile. Buds and whole tips of flower spikes are all excellent for colour and shape.

Wood Anemone *see* Anemone

Yarrow
Achillea millefolium White or pinkish. June-August. Press small sprays or single flowers. Small but very useful. Leaves good for shape.

Yellow Compositae
Senecio Yellow. July-September. A large family including the common ragwort, *Senecio jacobaea* Good colour but petals tend to shrivel. Press hard.

Yellow Melilot *see* Melilot

Trees

A number of trees have flowers which are suitable for pressing, and the following short list may be helpful.

Apple
Malus Pink/white. April-May. Press buds only. These will tend to turn brown, but the shape is good.

Elder
Sambucus nigra Cream/white. June-July. The flowers are excellent for pressing. The small buds dry a dark brown.

Hawthorn or May
Crataegus monogyna White. May-June. Flowers difficult to press when fully out. Press singly and in small sprays. (Pink May, single- and double-flowered varieties are also useful for pressing.)

Lime
Tilia Cream/yellow/green. July. Flowers and buds press well. Cut off some open flowers and press full face.

Ferns

Ferns of all sorts are excellent for pressing — size being the only governing factor! Press whole fronds or small single leaflets. The hart's-tongue fern, *Phyllitis vulgare*, is disappointing when dried, both in shape and colour.

Grasses

The members of the *Gramineae* family are nearly all rewarding to press. Beware the very thick types, such as bottle-grass, and those that are a bright silver white. Always try to pick grass when it is young and has just come into seed.

Lichens

Grey lichens found in damp areas can be used in flower pictures. The long feathery varieties should be pressed in small clusters and can be used effectively.

Mosses

These can also be pressed in very small pieces. The delicate fronds are useful, although the green colour sometimes fades to brown.

Rushes

Most members of the *Juncaceae* family will press satisfactorily and will look well in flower pictures. Do not pick old stems; the seeds will tend to drop off.

Sedges

Some of the varieties of the *Cyperaceae* family are thick and difficult to press. The smaller ones will be satisfactory.

Protected plants in the UK

The following wild flowers are protected by the Conservation of Wild Creatures and Wild Plants Act of 1975. It is an offence to remove any part of the plant.

Alpine gentian (*Gentiana nivalis*)
Alpine sow-thistle (*Cicerbita alpina*)
Alpine woodsia (*Woodsia alpina*)
Blue heath (*Phyllodoce caerulea*)
Cheddar pink (*Dianthus gratianopolitanus*)
Diapensia (*Diapensia lapponica*)
Drooping saxifrage (*Saxifraga cernua*)
Ghost orchid (*Epipogium aphyllum*)
Killarney fern (*Trichomanes speciosum*)
Lady's slipper (*Cypripedium calceolus*)
Mezereon (*Daphne mezereum*)
Military orchid (*Orchis militaris*)
Monkey orchid (*Orchis simia*)
Oblong woodsia (*Woodsia ilvensis*)
Red helleborine (*Cephalanthera rubra*)
Snowdon lily (*Lloydia serotina*)
Spiked speedwell (*Veronica spicata*)
Spring gentian (*Gentiana verna*)
Teesdale sandwort (*Minuartia stricta*)
Tufted saxifrage (*Saxifraga cespitosa*)
Wild gladiolus (*Gladiolus illyricus*)

Bibliography

Wild flowers

Martin, W. Keble, *Concise British Flora in Colour*, Michael Joseph, and Ebury Press, London, 1965

Fitter, Alistair and Richard, *Wild Flowers of Britain and Northern Europe*, Collins, London, 1974

Dealler, Stephen, *Wild Flowers for the Garden*, Batsford, London, 1977

Garden flowers

Hay, Roy and Synge, Patrick M., *Dictionary of Garden Plants in Colour*, Michael Joseph and Ebury Press (in collaboration with the Royal Horticultural Society), London, 1969

Anderson, E.B. etc., *Oxford Book of Garden Flowers*, Oxford University Press, Oxford, 1964

List of suppliers

Most of the products mentioned in this book are available from stationers and art shops. In case of difficulty, the following distributors may give advice on availability.

UK

Ready-cut cardboard mounts
Daler Board Co Ltd
Westminster Road
Wareham
Dorset BH20 4HT

Liquid gold paint
Connoisseur Studio (Europe) Ltd
PO Box 647
London W11

George Rowney & Co Ltd
Bracknell
Berks

USA

Drawing and cutting tools, coloured papers

Charrette (mail order)
2000 Mass Ave
Cambridge, Mass 02140

Framing tools and kits

Eubank Frame Inc
Salisbury
Maryland 21801

Twin City Moulding and Supply
2505 University Ave
St Paul, Minn 55114

Kulicke
636 Broadway
New York NY 10012

Index